CATHERINE TATE
TATE Laugh it Up!

First published in Great Britain in 2008 by

André Deutsch
an imprint of the
Carlton Publishing Group
20 Mortimer Street
London W1T 3JW

A CIP catalogue record for this book is available from the British Library

ISBN 978 0 233 00259 0

The publishers would like to thank the following sources for their kind
permission to reproduce the pictures in this book.

Page 1: (top) Peter Cook/View Pictures/Rex Features; (bottom) Dave M. Benett/Getty Images
Page 2: (top) ITV/Rex Features; (bottom) Dave Hogan/Getty Images
Page 3: (top) Ken McKay/Rex Features; (bottom) Ken McKay/Rex Features
Page 4: (top) Nils Jorgensen/Rex Features; (bottom) Richard Young/Rex Features
Page 5: (top) Huw John/Rex Features; (bottom) © Europa/Everett Collection/Rex Features
Page 6: (top) Giles Keyte/Working Title/The Kobal Collection; (bottom) ITV/Rex Features
Page 7: (top) Dave M. Benett/Getty Images; (bottom) Jon Furniss/WireImage/Getty Images
Page 8: Julian Makey/Rex Features

Every effort has been made to acknowledge correctly and contact the source and/or
copyright holder of each picture and Carlton Books Limited apologises for any unintentional
errors or omissions, which will be corrected in future editions of this book.

Typeset in Liverpool by E-Type
Printed and bound in the UK by CPI Mackays, Chatham, ME5 8TD

CATHERINE TATE
Laugh it Up!

The unauthorised
biography

TINA OGLE

ANDRE
DEUTSCH

Contents

Introduction

Speaking on *The Graham Norton Show* in the summer of 2008, when asked about her fame Catherine Tate said: 'I don't enjoy being Catherine Tate as much as my mother does.' She went on to relay how her mum's opening gambit to strangers is: 'Do you watch telly?' before launching into anecdotes about her famous daughter.

It was a funny comment, as befits this extremely talented comedienne, but it also sums up the 40-year-old's ambivalence towards her notoriety.

Anyone who is only familiar with Tate's work in her three eponymous series of sketch shows will no doubt be shocked to learn that she is far from brimming with confidence. Behind the extremely talented person we see on screen is a very complex individual who has battled with post-natal depression and shyness. That she conquered these and went on to become as famous and well loved as she is, is testament to the strength of her personality.

The fact that she wasn't an overnight success may well have helped her overcome her demons.

Fans only familiar with mouthy schoolgirl Lauren and her array of comedy counterparts will be unaware that Tate is actually a classically trained actress. Having tried for years, she eventually won a place at the prestigious Central School of Speech and Drama and then took small roles at the National Theatre and the Royal Shakespeare Company, as well as TV dramas before switching to stand-up comedy.

These years of struggle made Tate stronger and more able to cope with fame when it eventually arrived. She had met her partner Twig Clark and was pregnant with her daughter Erin when she started filming on the TV sitcom that would begin the process of making her public property. Playing opposite comedy legend Dawn French in *Wild West* introduced her to the world of press interviews. By the time the two series were over, she was hard at work perfecting the first series of *The Catherine Tate Show* and since then, she has never been out of the limelight or the headlines.

What is extraordinary is that she was deep into a bout of post-natal depression as she created the first of her own shows. Watching these with the benefit of hindsight, it's impossible to detect that the woman creating these gloriously funny and memorable characters was suffering at all.

Alongside the comedy that made her famous, Tate has also been mindful to branch out into other areas, lest she be seen as one-dimensional. While she's careful never to condemn the 'Am I bovvered?' catchphrase that brought her fame and fortune, it's obvious that she is desperate not to be remembered just for playing a stroppy 15-year-old schoolgirl, however hilarious. Roles in films have seen her name roll in the credits alongside such luminaries as Ewan McGregor, James McAvoy and Iain

Glen. She also famously played an ex-girlfriend of *Friends* star David Schwimmer in a play in the West End.

And, despite never having been a fan of that beloved behemoth of television that is sci-fi series *Doctor Who*, she took on the role of his assistant, Donna Noble, opposite the insanely popular David Tennant. This role, while heavily criticised by a certain section of rabid Whovians, made sure her face and name stayed in the spotlight and brought her a slew of new fans.

For the only child of a single parent family, raised on a council estate in the heart of London, it's been a fascinating journey. From being bullied at school, through temp jobs, drama school, tiny roles and success in the bearpit that is stand-up comedy, to national, mainstream recognition, she has stood her ground and tried never to play the fame game. Her alter ego, Lauren, has even been to Number 10 Downing Street to have cheeky exchanges with the then Prime Minister Tony Blair, as well as asking the Queen at a Royal Variety Performance, 'Is one bovvered?'

Whatever happens next, and given Tate's eclectic track record it will be interesting, her story so far is one that is more than worth reading. It should also provide inspiration to anyone who isn't filled with self-confidence but who secretly believes they could make their mark through persistence, hard work and native talent.

Tina Ogle

CHAPTER ONE

The Only Child

In a tiny flower shop down a quaint alley in Bloomsbury, central London, signed photographs of a beaming Catherine Tate compete for prominence with the beautiful range of blooms on offer. While a casual visitor might be surprised to find the award-winning actress and comedian on display here, grinning happily with her arm around former Prime Minister Tony Blair, it has been her mother's place of business for more than forty years.

Her mother and various family members still run the shop, which specializes in beautifully wrought arrangements and friendly, informal service. If you're seeking something to enhance your dinner table, they'll happily discuss whether the smell of the individual flowers will compete with your food and even offer to lend you a vase – 'Where do you live, dear? Oh, just bring it back when you can. Now, which one would you like?'

Small wonder then that Catherine Tate, born Catherine Ford on May 12, 1968, and brought up on the nearby Brunswick Council Estate, is fiercely proud of her background and particularly her mother Josephine, whose creative skills have kept this business afloat for more than four decades. Catherine may now hobnob with prime ministers and monarchs, and herself be deemed comedy royalty, but it is in this small florist that she first learned how the world worked. As she told *The Independent*: 'I'm the only child and it's only now that I've got my own TV show that Mum is beginning to realize I'm not going to join the business.'

It may have taken Catherine a long time to become an overnight success but, with the launch of *The Catherine Tate Show* on BBC2 in 2004, she very quickly became public property. And as the former convent schoolgirl catapulted to fame as one of Britain's funniest women and sharpest observers of human nature, much has been written about her apparently humble origins.

The product of a very happy but fatherless home, she is extremely quick to defend what she has described as an idyllic upbringing. As she told *The Guardian,* with a palpable sense of indignation: 'It makes better copy doesn't it? I remember sitting with a journalist and her having this fantasy in her head "Oh, it's Eliza Doolittle." And I said, "No, it's not actually. That wasn't my experience. I had the most fantastic childhood".'

So no *My Fair Lady* rags to riches tale then, whatever journalists desperate for an easily recognizable story would like to think. Rather it was a steady rise from stable and loving beginnings, and no less fascinating for its failure to conform to a fairytale formula.

Brought up by her mother, who chose to leave her father before Catherine was six months old, and her grandmother and godmother, Catherine grew up in the heart of London on a council estate within walking distance of the famous neighbourhoods of Covent Garden and the West End. Now given a £24m facelift, the Brunswick Centre has been transformed, painted cream and softened into a trendy shopping complex, housing businesses such as Starbucks and the Italian deli Carluccio's, clothes shops such as Oasis and L.K. Bennett and that ultimate in middle-class luxury, a Waitrose supermarket. Council tenants still live in the updated flats, some of which now exchange hands for up to half a million pounds. And they do grumble, somewhat understandably, about their old, reliable Safeway being replaced by the upmarket and pricey Waitrose.

Back in the 1960s it was a fairly brutal and very grey-looking, low-rise complex. Even when Catherine was growing up there though, it was surrounded by universities and bookshops and the legacy of Virginia Woolf, and carried the whiff of Bohemia. Novelist Woolf and her publisher husband Leonard were at the heart of a group of intellectuals known as 'the Bloomsbury Set' in the early part of the twentieth century. This group, that included the novelist E.M. Forster, influential economist John Maynard Keynes and biographer Lytton Strachey, gave the area an intellectual identity that lingers to this day. Given that, and its proximity to London's rich cultural life, it was certainly not a terrible place in which to spend one's childhood.

Catherine talks proudly of Leicester Square and Covent Garden being 'just around the corner', and being able to see art house movies at the Renoir Cinema which was part of her estate, while in her late teens she hung out at the world famous London Comedy Store and walked home alone late at night. At the time the Comedy Store was located in Leicester Square, though it has now moved around the corner to Oxenden Street, and was a hugely influential proving ground for new comic talent. Raucous, rowdy and famous for its drunken but often effective hecklers, it was the best gig to get if you wanted to hone your skills and be noticed. This was where the 'alternative comedy' scene began in the early 1980s and launched the careers of *The Young Ones* Rik Mayall and Adrian Edmondson, as well as Ben Elton and Alexei Sayle. A young Catherine Tate used to see Sayle riding around her area on his bike, and he later became a big fan of her brand of comedy, even interviewing her for the *Radio Times*. Having watched the best comedians of her generation prove themselves in this often hostile environment, she at least knew what she was getting into somewhat later in her life.

As an only child, Catherine was certainly cosseted and has described being 'idolized' by this coterie of women who looked out for her every need. As she told the *Sunday Mirror*: 'My nan and my godmother looked after me when Mum was working. They were very cautious with me and I was scared of most things. My school report said "Catherine worries a lot." I remember Mum telling Nan, "You've got to let her come down the slide on her own!"'

It is this close circle of women that she credits with giving her the confidence and humour to succeed as spectacularly as she has to date. 'It was very matriarchal,' she told the *Radio Times*. 'I had my mum, my nan and my godmother and they were all very, very funny women. I look back now and think "God, they gave me so much material." I absolutely know that I wouldn't be doing what I was doing now if I hadn't had that background.'

She attended Saint Joseph's Catholic primary school in Holborn, a mere hop, skip and a jump from her mother's flower shop and was reportedly very happy there. She has lovingly described, too, wonderful pageants in her home which could really only have been enacted in the 1970s.

Many other daughters of this peculiar decade will no doubt recognize her description of re-enacting her Miss World winner's speech every year. 'Can you believe it? Every year, I'd go out onto the landing when they were announcing the top three, then I'd come into the living room, first as the runners-up and then as the winner, shedding a suitable tear while my mum and my nan clapped.' It's hard to believe it now, but this worldwide beauty contest was then a fixture of the television schedules. Genial host Michael Aspel would interview all the contestants about their home countries and their 'ambitions' for the future – with halting answers being essayed in broken English. Who won and who should have won was then discussed at length in the playground the next day. Similar scenes would ensue on a weekly basis as she forced her mum to announce her as the different contestants on Hughie Green's *Opportunity Knocks*. An innocent forerunner to the likes of *Britain's Got Talent*, this showcased everyone from singing miners to fresh-faced poppets with a yen to be on television. Green, who later turned out to be the real father of Paula Yates, used the catchphrase 'And I mean that most sincerely' but even at a very young age you knew that he didn't.

Television, even then, was obviously an important part of her life, which just goes to show that even access to just three channels, as was the case when Catherine was growing up, can stimulate the creative imagination of a child. At the time, there was only BBC1, BBC2 and ITV and they only broadcast for limited hours with a nightly shutdown: no 24-hour television and very limited daytime shows. Because of these limitations, programmes were watched by many more millions of viewers and were big events in people's lives. Being exposed to 1970s classics such as *The Two Ronnies* and *The Morecambe And Wise Show* surely influenced Tate's concept of comedy and gave her a grounding to go on and develop her own.

Catherine says that then she had no idea she wanted to go into show business, but her early mimicking of TV contestants for her family must have come in useful as practice. Her chameleon nature was evident to her even then: 'I've always been changeable. When I was a child, there would be days when I didn't want to be called Catherine. I'd be someone else entirely.' Life as she describes it was certainly lots of fun and it was only when she moved to Notre Dame High School in Southwark at the age of eleven that things took a slightly darker turn. A Catholic school south of the Thames, Notre Dame had been in existence since it was set up by the sisters of Notre Dame in 1855. Known as a centre of excellence, part of its mission statement reads: 'It strives to educate women to reach their full potential, to be confident, to be successful and to become mature and responsible citizens.' But making the journey to a new area and with new school mates, Catherine was suddenly shy, and self-conscious about her red hair, and became the victim of bullying. 'When I was at an all-girls' convent school, I was emotionally and mentally bullied in the way only teenage girls can be. I used to go red when anybody spoke to me. It's awful because you absolutely cannot control it. If you are a child that blushes, or is shy, the one thing you want in the world is to be the child who comes in and says, "hi", to everyone and goes up and makes friends.'

It seems extremely likely it was during this turbulent, teenage time that she first realized she could use humour and a facility for characterisation to her advantage. If the red-headed, blushing, painfully shy Catherine wasn't enough to impress this strange and unyielding bunch of girls, then perhaps an armour of comedy would protect her. As she told *The Daily Telegraph*: 'I realized if I got myself some sort of label or persona to hide behind, that would get me, the real me, out of the spotlight. There was, I'll always remember, one defining moment when I was thirteen and had just come back from the dentist. A girl came running up and said, "Come on then, tell us", and I suddenly realized, ah, great, they expect me to put a spin on this... now how about if I give the dentist a voice...'

The then thirteen-year-old Catherine could surely have never dreamt that this first caricature of a man who had just worked on her teeth would be the beginning of a career that would make her hugely famous and much-loved. Nor could she have suspected that the bullies who tormented her, wherever they ended up, couldn't fail to be aware of her enormous success in later life. She'd have to be a very forgiving person not to take even some small pleasure from this very public turnaround in fortunes.

Yet, despite this dentist story, she's also been quick to point out that she wasn't parading around the playground attracting attention by putting on funny voices and creating prototypes for filthy Nan and teen rebel Lauren. In fact, the idea of attempting to draw so much attention to herself seems to horrify her. 'I wasn't some sort of walking variety act around school. I think my circle of friends would have said I'm funny, but I wasn't a class jester. Because I was a shy and awkward child I used humour to deflect attention. It was a controlling mechanism. I could use it to control my image.'

The themes of shyness and control are ones that come up again and again when she's interviewed. It seems that a self-conscious child grew up to be a very shy adult, despite the very public career that she chose to pursue. Never very comfortable in the limelight, she admits that she learnt to hide her real self from a very early age and that it was a very deliberate strategy. 'Oh, I am very calculated… But it was subconscious. At fourteen, I don't think you can be that Machiavellian. But when I realized I had a facility for humour, I latched onto it, and it gave me confidence and I built my personality around it. So I subconsciously made myself become the funny one so that would be my label rather than the ginger one or the red-faced one.'

There is a really sweet picture of her at around age five, with a halo of red curls, half-smiling self-consciously at the camera, that she chose to share with the *Sunday Mirror* back in 2005. As she explained then: 'My mum always kept my hair short as a child. She obviously liked people thinking I was a boy. Even when I was in skirts, people would say, "Why have you got that little boy in a dress?"'

Even as she jokes about it so effectively now, her tomboy image obviously had a detrimental effect. In the same *Sunday*

Mirror piece, there's another photo from her personal collection. Here, aged thirteen, she's clutching a newspaper to her stomach and peeking out shyly from what was unmistakably a Princess Di haircut, *circa* the early 1980s. Newly engaged to Prince Charles, Lady Diana as she then was, was a hugely influential figure for young girls – just about everyone wanted to emulate the princess in waiting. A combed forward bob with a shaped nape of neck, the style was a continuation of the one popularized by Joanna Lumley as crime-fighting Purdey in the popular drama series *The New Avengers*. The pie crust collars and jersey V neck sleeveless pullovers she sported were also best sellers at the time. You couldn't escape the look.

'This was my Princess Di stage. I was thirteen and I remember thinking I really looked like her. Mum and I were in Crete, and, despite the fact it was eighty degrees outside, I wouldn't go anywhere without my Benetton jumper. All I did on this beautiful island was stay in my room, listening to the Kids from *Fame* with the blinds closed. My poor mum. I remember being quite shy back then. It's ironic, considering what I do now. I didn't want to act at that age. My main goal at the time was to marry Prince Andrew. Or be a ski instructor.'

She might well have been in with a chance with Prince Andrew if she'd stuck it out, given that he ended up with another famous redhead in a relationship that very publicly didn't pan out. Instead, in one of the cheekiest, most talked about Royal Variety Performances of all time, she ended up asking his mother 'Is one bovvered?' But more of that, and Prince Philip's possible objections to Tate as a future daughter-in-law, later.

She's given more insight into her childhood anxieties by describing a strange habit involving word association. Apparently, on going to bed, she couldn't possibly leave her jumper on the floor as jumper began with a 'J' as did her mother's name, Josephine, and she thought bad things would happen to her mother if she left it lying in a heap. As she told *The Guardian*: 'I had one thing – see, your coat is on the floor... I'd think, "Oh, coat begins with 'C'", then I would think of someone I knew whose name began with "C" who I would hate to see crumpled on the floor and then I'd have to pick it up. So it was quite debilitating for a short amount of time.' She's very keen to stress that it was a short-lived problem, however, and that she isn't forced to observe the same sort of rituals today.

Even despite these fairly natural childhood and teenage anxieties though, she was clearly not someone totally consumed by angst. Surrounded by people who idolized her, and given all the comforts her hard-working mother could provide, she enjoyed a standard of living she considers very special indeed.

While not wealthy, her mother sounds like an eminently sensible woman, who deemed cheap haircuts and cheap face creams a false economy. She also took Catherine on foreign holidays every year to places such as Greece, Portugal and Spain. Even if Catherine did decide to spend most of the time indoors, sheltering from the sunshine, listening to TV soundtracks and dreaming of joining the Royal Family.

Describing herself as 'sheltered', she endearingly found herself totally perplexed by a chippy attitude she encountered at school. It seems strange and old-fashioned that she never harboured any resentment to those financially better off than herself, but it's obviously testament to a very healthy upbringing. As she told *The Guardian*: 'A teacher had gone to Barbados for her honeymoon, and when she came back one of the kids said to her, "It's OK for some." I had never heard that before. I went home and asked my mum what it meant, and she said, "Oh, it's just a saying, but always remember, we are the some." By a lot of people's standards, I lived a very privileged life. I never wanted for attention, I never wanted for material things. In some ways, I was probably spoiled because I never had to share. And I was doted on.'

As well as her deep and abiding connection with her family, she also feels herself very much to be a Londoner, and is protective of both the area and the city she grew up and still lives in. And even though her sketch show characters have universal appeal – *Friends* star David Schwimmer says that Nan kills him – they all have their roots very firmly buried in the capital city. It's no surprise then that she slightly turns her nose up at those people who have merely chosen to live in London but come from elsewhere. 'I don't want to sound like some leg-cocking Cockney,' she told the *Radio Times*, "but there is a difference between people who are *from* London and people who just live here. Non-Londoners think where I grew up in Bloomsbury is all just bookshops and hotels, but it's a community with its own life and language.'

She goes on to describe how she first saw the world she grew up in depicted beautifully in the multi-award winning, smash-hit sitcom *Only Fools And Horses*. Written by fellow Londoner John Sullivan, the show came as a major revelation to a girl who grew up on posh BBC costume dramas, received pronunciation and Aga-sagas. Initially receiving very poor viewing figures, *Only Fools And Horses* was repeated at the last minute and went on to become a huge hit and a national institution. Its main character Del Boy Trotter (David Jason) became a rough diamond icon while his hapless brother Rodney (Nicholas Lyndhurst) was equally loved. Telling the tall tales of an extended family living in a council flat and ducking and diving in order to survive, it struck a chord in Thatcher's Britain. Its catchphrases such as 'cushty' and 'lovely jubbly' also went on to be shouted across the nation. Anyone familiar with the Trotter's psychedelic living room in a flat on a Peckham council estate in *Only Fools* would feel at home in the residence of Tate's outrageous character 'Nan'.

'I couldn't believe there were people speaking like us on the telly. We'd been using phrases like "cushty" for generations, but people thought it was a catchphrase invented for the programme. I really admired the writer, John Sullivan, for finding something of his own that he found funny, and having the confidence to believe that other people would find it funny too.'

Given the racial, cultural and geographical diversity of television output today, it's difficult to believe that a working class London sitcom like *Only Fools And Horses* could have such a dramatic effect on a young Londoner. But seeing Del Boy, Rodney and Grandpa brought to life certainly seems to have made Catherine realize that it was possible that she too might one day be allowed to find her voice on national television.

Dreams of marrying into royalty or teaching yahoos how to negotiate the slopes of Switzerland aside, there was eventually something that drew Catherine to drama. However, her first encounter with the great dramatic texts proved to be a deeply unfulfilling one. Being surrounded by all those bookshops had its effect though, and she found herself browsing through a very august establishment. Located in Fitzroy Street, very close to her home, Samuel French has been publishing, leasing and selling plays for performance since 1830 and is the leader in its field. It also has a bookshop selling the texts of plays and books on all aspects of theatre, and is very grand in an old-fashioned way.

'Samuel French, the famous drama publishers, was just around the corner. I went down there one day, and picked up a copy of *Three Sisters* by Chekhov. I read it and just thought, "This is rubbish. Really boring, terrible rubbish!" Then, a few months later I saw the play on stage and was transfixed. I simply couldn't understand how they'd turned those words I'd dismissed into what I had just seen on stage. That was the moment I first felt the pull of the theatre.'

Those only familiar with her award-winning sketch series *The Catherine Tate Show* may not realize that serious acting was her initial ambition and the talent that brought her to the public eye in the first place. Her desire to explore the theatre also got her away from the difficult all-girls' convent school. Although having first been bullied there, she'd used her humour to develop a role as a natural ringleader – 'I was probably just trying to work a crowd' – and was considered something of a rebel. She even ended up enjoying her time at school, claiming: 'Me and my friends laughed from the moment we got there until the moment we left.' It is probably here that the seeds of the ultimate stroppy teenager Lauren 'Am I bovvered?' Cooper were planted, even though it would take the best part of 20 years for her to strut her way into the spotlight and become a national obsession.

At sixteen then, having announced her intentions and ambitions to become an actress, the nuns told Catherine she would have to move to a different school, as they simply didn't have the resources to provide her with the education she needed. She was transferred to an all boys' school, Salesian College, Battersea in South London. Run on the educational principles of a nineteenth-century priest Saint John Bosco, this was another strict Catholic school. Bosco had founded hostels and boarding schools to teach underprivileged young boys in Italy in the mid-nineteenth century and went on to found the Salesian Society religious order in 1854. Its influence still stretches worldwide to this day. It must have been an enormous shock to these cloistered boys when a handful of girls appeared to brighten up their single sex existence. What made it auspicious for Catherine was that when she turned up on the first day, she didn't have a uniform. This early 1980s fashion moment proved to be a turning point in young Catherine's life. 'I was wearing these checked trousers – I really loved them. I walked into the playground and three hundred boys ran towards me shouting, "Rupert the Bear!" That was it, I was Rupert for the rest of my time there. I was a celebrity. It got to the point where I needed an escort. There would be third-years coming up in the library and prodding me, because I was a girl.' She later said she felt like Kylie Minogue and it was an important boost in self-esteem for the self-confessed blushing misfit.

So, like most of us, Catherine Tate had a childhood of happy memories mixed with anxieties. There may not have been a father figure in her life, but she doesn't seem to have suffered from that. As she told *The Observer*: 'I've never been driven by a desire for approval because I've never lacked approval. My family worshipped me when I was young.'

However, she has admitted that she found it difficult having a man telling her what to do as in her early world it was always the women who made the rules. 'I remember once a male supply teacher coming into school and telling me to sit down. I thought, "What? Who are you? How dare you?" Because in my head it was women who disciplined me and had any rights to tell me what to do.' As any fan of her sketch show will recognize, there are definite shades of Lauren in that vividly remembered scenario.

She is also rendered near speechless with rage at inaccurate reports that her father left her and her mother rather than the other way around: 'It actually makes me gag to say it. My mum rang up and said she'd just seen an interview where it said, "Dad left me and Mum", and I just thought, "Oh you... oh you... you..." I hate all that "Dad" and "Mum". I wouldn't be that informal – I'd never say that. Actually it was the other way round. My mum left my father. It was a decision to leave.'

She has never named her father or, apparently, had any contact with him whatsoever. Her attitude suggests that this is something she would never do. Given her very public success, it's perhaps surprising that he hasn't emerged or been dug out by the tabloids, anxious for any whiff of scandal or personal interest story about a major star.

So, adored by her family, at times painfully shy, funny with her peers, intrigued by theatre and with a new surge of confidence from her stint at an all-male school, Catherine Tate left school without sitting her A levels, intent on being accepted at drama school and finding her way as a serious actress.

CHAPTER TWO

First Jobs and Drama School

Catherine Tate must have been very sure about her vocation as an actress as she decided to leave Salesian College, Battersea, without taking her A levels. Having realized that she didn't need them to get into drama school, she decided there was no point in putting herself through the pain of intensive exams. But this ambition to become an actress wasn't born out of a sense of overwhelming confidence, far from it. As she later told *The Daily Telegraph*: 'It wasn't easy for me because I was very shy, cripplingly shy. But I just knew I had to do it.'

A stint in youth theatre had helped seal her ambitions, making her feel more confident in front of an audience. She has since described this experience as 'a building block for personality', adding, 'Being able to make people laugh immediately made me feel confident and other people think I was confident.'

Getting into costume and a different persona also built on her technique of disguising herself through humour. 'I think performing for me was a way of a shy child deflecting attention away from herself. If I could dress up and pretend to be someone else...'

Early theatrical experiences included appearing in a Shakespearean production in London's West End. 'I think I was seven when I appeared in Drury Lane in a Shakespeare play. I can't remember the production, but I had to run on stage and nick an apple and I remember thinking, "What are they saying?" It sounded like a different language.' The theatre itself, the Theatre Royal on Drury Lane, is also likely to have made a big impression on a wide-eyed youngster. An elaborate and beautifully designed space, it holds an audience of over three thousand people. The current theatre was built in 1812 but there has been a theatre on the site since 1663, and it has a long and illustrious history. Shakespearean actor Edmund Kean, considered the greatest actor of his time in the early nineteenth century, forged his career there and even the cult comedy troupe Monty Python recorded a concert album there. It is currently owned by impresario Andrew Lloyd Webber and usually stages big musical productions.

This increased confidence and her desire to find out more about this exciting, if incomprehensible, world led her to apply to a famous theatre school, a mere five minutes' walk from her home. The fiercely competitive Sylvia Young Stage School has hot-housed such well-known British talents as former *EastEnders* Tamzin Outhwaite, Letitia Dean, Dean Gaffney and Lacey Turner, as well as Spice Girl Emma Bunton, *Ashes To Ashes* actress Keeley Hawes, Denise Van Outen and *X Factor* winner and now global superstar Leona Lewis. However, it took Catherine just a week, she has said, to realize that she was 'no Bonnie Langford'. It is interesting then that she would later go on to use this former child star as a guest in *The Catherine Tate Show*. In another coincidence Langford also played an assistant to Doctor Who back in 1986/87. As Mel, a bubbly keep-fit fanatic who tried to convert the Doctor to exercise and carrot juice, she was one of the least popular assistants but worked with both Sylvester McCoy and Colin Baker. Perhaps the two have compared notes over their occasional maulings from rabid Whovians?

Catherine left Sylvia Young's and applied to the Central School of Speech and Drama only to be turned down.

She decided to use this lull in proceedings to go to Spain for the best part of a year, working both as a nanny and selling time shares in apartments. How such a shy girl still in her teens managed to flog such a notoriously difficult product is not recorded. It's possible that she developed some alter ego to pull off the task. After all, you can't imagine walking away without signing something if Nan were to give you her ultimate sales pitch, liberally spattered with 'f' words and all.

Her own nan, however, who had been used to seeing her granddaughter every day since birth, was very upset when Catherine went off to foreign shores at this time. As Tate told *The Observer*: 'When I was eighteen I lived in Spain for a bit, and she literally took to her bed until I got back.'

Some eight years later, when she wanted to move across London to Fulham in the west, she ended up not telling her grandmother for fear that it would upset her. When the prospect was first mooted, her nan had said: 'Don't do that, darlin', it'll make me ill if you move away.' It was only six months later that she confessed that she had done it anyway. 'She was horrified,' said Tate, 'even though I'd still seen her every day!"

*

The next few years were taken up with temp work as Tate kept on applying to the Central School, hoping that they would eventually recognize her talent and say 'yes'. She was rejected three years in a row and, to have kept the faith for this long and not given up, must have taken a certain stubborn self-belief. She might have been a sensitive flower but she certainly wasn't going to let a little thing like a rejection from a major theatre school ruin her dreams.

'I tried four times to get into the Central School of Speech and Drama before I got accepted. They used to get me down to the last four every year and I was just about to say, "OK, forget it", when they let me in. I started when I was seventeen, which was too young, in retrospect, and finally went when I was twenty-one. I just kept plugging away. Determined? Yeah, I think I was.' Central can rightly lay claim to being one of the finest drama schools in the country. It's illustrious alumni include veteran greats such as Peggy Ashcroft and Laurence Olivier, former Doctor Who Peter Davison, national institution Dame Judi Dench, modern favourite James Nesbitt, as well as Jennifer Saunders and Dawn French. Tate would later go on to make her television breakthrough starring opposite French, though their paths never crossed at Central. She did meet her sketch show co-writer Derren Litten here though, and he also starred in *The Catherine Tate Show*.

Her audition piece was based on something she saw actor Ian McKellen do in a one-man Shakespeare show years earlier. 'It had audience interaction and I leapt at the chance to die on stage with Ian McKellen. He recited a war speech and I got into drama school on the back of it. I made it the basis of my audition.' She was obviously good at spotting talent early as Ian McKellen went on to be knighted for his fine acting work in 1991.

However, it seems that her time at drama school wasn't all fulfilled ambitions and jolly japes. Having admitted to being transfixed by the Kids from *Fame* as a child, at least a tiny part of her must have thought that life at the Central might be like that American drama – 'Fame costs, and this is where you start paying' – and jumping onto the roof of yellow taxis to put on the show right here.

She was sceptical of some of the excessive 'luvviness' that she saw around her – as well she might be, coming from the background that she did. 'I'd spend more time making people laugh at drama school than I'd spend applying myself to "my art". At Central there was a certain amount of animal study and "let's all give each other massages" and I thought, "Oh my God, please don't tell me this is what it's all about. People are *dying* in the world. And we're just hugging."' This slightly detached attitude must have made her feel a bit of an outsider, a theme repeated from her secondary school days, but she seems sanguine about the experience now: 'I guess I was a little bit cynical but that's what being a student is.'

Her ambition was to be a serious actress and she was disappointed on leaving in 1993 that opportunities seemed to be so few and far between: 'It's what I went to drama school for and I honestly thought I would come out and do plays, but it was 1993 and there was no rep.'

Repertory theatre, so popular in England in the middle part of the twentieth century, had all but died out by the time Tate was looking for gainful employment. The repertory movement began in the early twentieth century and was designed so that as wide an audience as possible would be exposed to different types of theatre at an affordable price. Famous repertory theatres included the Gaiety Theatre in Manchester, the Birmingham Repertory Theatre and the Citizens in Glasgow. A funding crisis in the 1980s put paid to a large part of the repertory world but some theatres survive to this day. It would seem that she was in love with the idea of a tightly knit group of thespians adopting different parts in different plays as they toured across the country. Even after her success in television and films she said: 'I'd love to be part of J.B. Priestley's Good Companions – a merry troupe of people schlepping round the country.'

But it was not to be and she was pushed into the modern day equivalent of repertory theatre – bit parts in long-running TV dramas such as *The Bill* and *Casualty*.

You'd have to have very sharp eyes and a long memory to recall her as 'girlfriend' in hospital drama *Surgical Spirit*, 'young woman' in popular sitcom *Men Behaving Badly*, or a PA in the long-forgotten Mel Smith legal drama *Milner*. She popped up twice in *The Bill*, once in 1993 as Woman Detective Constable Palmer and then as Karen Brogan in 1994. Presumably no-one noticed the difference. She was also Ginnie Readman in one episode of the long-running fire-fighting drama *London's Burning.*

She also worked at the Oxford Stage Company for a while, as well as having small parts with the National Theatre and the Royal Shakespeare Company – mostly as servants and spear-carriers as is often the case with young, unknown actors. Not having the traditional good looks to land leading lady parts, she was realistic about her dramatic options from an early age. 'You come out of drama school and if you're very lucky you get into a select stream of romantic leads, but I kind of knew that wouldn't happen to me.'

However, she soldiered on, mixing whatever acting work she could get with more office work, the latter surely providing her with the research for such work-based characters in her sketch show as 'How Much/How Many' and 'Last Hit Woman'. Again, she seemed fairly philosophical about this state of affairs, telling *The Times*: 'If you're just coming out of drama school, unless you're plucked in the third year for a lead part, you have to work your way through. I did other jobs. I did office work, and I had such a great time in the meantime. When the roll stops in theatre, some people are at a loss, but I liked it.'

She claims to have been utterly useless at secretarial work though, having no shorthand, lacking any organizational skills whatsoever and being totally at sea when it came to computers. The funniest story she tells about these days of being on call as a temporary secretary involves a very well-known computer operating system. When one employer asked her if she did Windows, she thought he meant the see-through kind rather than the

Microsoft version and took umbrage: 'I thought it was a bit much and said they were too high.' One can only imagine Bill Gates's reaction to this comical misunderstanding. He may have achieved global domination but his ideas had obviously not reached that part of Catherine Tate's brain.

She was unhappy too at the National Theatre, seeing no way of progressing beyond the tiny parts she was being offered. This very prestigious institution on the South Bank of the Thames includes three theatres, the largest being the Olivier Theatre, named after the National's first artistic director Sir Laurence Olivier. Slightly smaller is the Lyttelton, followed by the studio space of the Cottesloe Theatre. The building, an example of Brutalist architecture, has been the subject of much debate. Prince Charles said of it in 1988: "A clever way of building a nuclear power station in the middle of London without anyone objecting." Their mission is to put on Shakespeare's work as well as other classics and new plays by some of our foremost writers. The artistic director when Tate was there was Richard Eyre, and his track record of hits included Tom Stoppard's *Arcadia*, *Sweeney Todd* and a trilogy of David Hare plays. But Tate found that she wasn't being offered roles that stretched her in any way.

'There were three people marked down for success at my drama school. The problem at the National was that there was no way to move out of playing these tiny parts. That's why I switched to stand-up comedy – if you're an unemployed actor, you're waiting for the phone to ring, whereas as a comic you're in control, you can just go out and do a gig somewhere.'

We'll explore her switch to stand-up comedy in more depth

later, but it was most certainly a response to the lack of success she was experiencing as a jobbing actress. When she failed to get a part in a Royal Court production, the prestigious theatre based in London's Sloane Square, losing the role to someone she knew well, she began to doubt the wisdom of her career choice. 'A friend got the part instead and I remember thinking, "This is not going to happen." I was very worried, restless and discontented. When I was twenty-six my mother said, "You could have been working in a bank for five years now."'

Luckily for comedy fans, she didn't bolt for the nearest Job Centre and apply to work behind the counter at HSBC but instead switched her attention and efforts to stand-up comedy. It might have been her heartfelt and life-long belief in astrology that kept her keeping on. In her birth chart, she read the rather dire warning: 'Strive to be successful because you'll be a very bitter failure.' As she admitted later on: 'That stuck with me.' Given her continued success, hopefully neither she nor the rest of the world will come to find out whether that prophecy would have come true.

It's good to know, too, that despite her disillusionment with the way the theatrical hierarchy worked, she never lost her passion for the stage. She played feisty servant Smeraldina in an RSC production of Carlo Goldoni's *A Servant With Two Masters*, which toured the world in 2001 and got great reviews, before making the move into television, which must have helped. She also met her life partner Twig Clark while on this world tour with the RSC, another rather large endorsement for the roar of the greasepaint and the smell of the crowd. Clark was a stage

25

manager on the tour and they sealed their romance in Western Australia as she later explained: "We got together at Margaret River. It's beautiful. We just rented a place by the beach when we had a week off."

She also sealed her commitment to the art of the stage in December 2006 by becoming the patron of the Royal Court Theatre's high-profile and much sought-after Young Writers' Festival. Others to have held this mentoring position have included Kathy Burke, Ray Winstone and Hanif Kureishi, all of whom have high profiles and great track records so she was in excellent company.

Tate certainly had no reservations: 'When they asked my agent, I told her to jump on it. We forget we need to invest in the writing of plays, when really the playwright is the most important person in the process.'

She saw in her involvement a way of making the theatre much more accessible to those less privileged, an issue dear to her own heart. 'I'm over the moon they considered me over someone who writes indecipherable plays – and we do walk among people who write indecipherable plays. Theatre is always supposed to have been for the masses. To produce something that is alienating is as great a crime as to produce something that is not entertaining. I want to help young people write things that are easy to understand. Who wants to leave a theatre going, "Hmm, that was interesting"?'

It must have been wonderful, too, to receive such an endorsement from the highly respected theatre that had turned her down for a role at such a crucial stage in her career. Thank goodness for her Taurean stubborn streak and her faith in the stars. Without that powerful combination, we may never have had the comedy pleasure of Catherine Tate.

But these wilderness years also left her with her feet firmly on the ground. As she said only recently: 'I've spent longer in temp work than working in TV.' With these sobering thoughts in her head, it's unlikely she'll ever get carried away leading the celebrity high life.

CHAPTER THREE

Stand-up Comedy

As a teenager, Catherine Tate only lived a fifteen-minute walk away from the Comedy Store in London's Leicester Square. Here, back in the 1980s, some of the best performers of their generation were cutting their comedy teeth in nightly shows, both improvisation and stand-up.

When she was still in the sixth form, Tate used to wander down to this hot-bed of comic talent and watch closely all that was on offer. Walking home late at night, she can only have dreamed of one day taking to the stage there herself.

But any definite comedy ambitions she had didn't crystallize till much later. She was set on becoming a serious actress and, as we have seen, temped her way through four years of trying to be accepted at stage school.

It was only after having completed the course she had dreamt of at the Central School of Speech and Drama, and having spent several years trying to make an impact in dramatic roles, that her thoughts turned to stand-up as a way of getting herself noticed. Frustrated and bored with tiny roles in television dramas and sporadic theatre work, she was looking for a new challenge. 'I wanted to do more. I was looking at stand-up, thinking I'd like a go at that. I thought if nothing happens, I'll just get on with my life.'

For a self-confessed shy person and teetotaller, putting herself on stage in front of dozens of drunk and rowdy comedy fans to be judged would seem like a very peculiar career choice. And she has admitted as much: 'I know, it's extraordinary. And you know, it's a preposterous idea – you're asking people who don't know you to a) be quiet, b) listen to what you say, and c) laugh. But if I'd never done stand-up, I would have been disappointed with myself. The excitement drew me too much – it was a delicious danger.'

So there's obviously an adrenaline junkie buried not too deeply in Tate's psyche – why else would she put herself though such a trial by fire? But her disappointment and frustration at the lack of direction in her acting career can't be underestimated either. As she said later: 'If I hadn't taken the plunge I'd probably still be playing whores and servants for nothing and sitting by the telephone waiting for *The Bill* to call.' Having already been Woman Detective Constable Palmer *and* Karen Brogan in that particular cop series, her options were fast running out.

It was just as well then that she took to this fairly dangerous pastime almost immediately: 'I was much happier straight away. Very, very happy.'

What seems even stranger, given her history of shyness and being bullied, was that she actively liked the confrontational nature of stand-up. 'I really did like the gladiatorial aspect of it – if it was a particularly rough club you would get a bit of trouble. I like the fact that people wanted to have a go. There's an arrogance involved in doing stand-up comedy because what you're saying is, "Yeah, have a go, but know this, I believe I'm funnier than you", and when the audience gets behind you and acknowledges that, it's brilliant. You need a kamikaze instinct because it's stupid, really – it's just that the reward is too great.'

It wouldn't take a leading psychiatrist to suggest that conquering hecklers was perhaps her way of getting her own back on the bullies who had made some of her school days so miserable. If she could whip these cocky men and women who wanted to put her down a peg or two into line, the future must have seemed like a much safer place.

What also appealed to her very much was the feeling that stand-up comedy was something that the stand-up comic puts the work into and then reaps the rewards. Rather than being something you swanned into from Oxford or Cambridge, or got an entrée into because Daddy knew someone, stand-up comedy was an arena where only the best and the toughest could survive.

As she told fellow stand-up comedian Alexei Sayle, one of the pioneers of alternative comedy in the 1980s: 'What I love about stand-up is that it's a time-served apprenticeship – you have to learn how to do it over a period of years – and it's tough, there's no room for deluding yourself.'

When faced with an audience full of stony faces and a dreadful silence, even the most bumptious of characters would have problems convincing themselves that they were right and the audience wrong. For most of us, the thought of putting ourselves through being judged like this is utterly horrifying. For Tate though, it was an experience that she kept on repeating to build up her reserves of self-belief. And she knew exactly what the risks were. 'You have to be immediately funny in stand-up. It doesn't matter if you think your stuff is clever or well-observed, if they don't laugh, it's all over – they're not going to go home and think about it afterwards. I liked that pressure of going out there – it has an amazing effect on your confidence.'

While it's an extremely high-risk method of confidence building, and most definitely not recommended for the faint-hearted or fumbling, it clearly paid dividends for Tate. She kept on doing open-mic spots until she got booked under her own name and very slowly built up a small following.

*

This careful inching towards recognition was a very deliberate strategy on her part. She had long realized that television companies were paying very close attention to the stand-up circuit at that time, and were drawing many of their future stars from its small but growing circle. As she later said: 'It seemed to be at the time that stand-up was very big. I don't know why, but people tend to look at stand-ups and think they can act, which actually isn't the case. But never mind. I thought, if that's the area where they're looking, then that's the area that I'll put myself – even as a means to an end. And it was.'

This does sound very calculating and who can blame her? Yet for someone who at times has claimed not to be ambitious, it seems to sit oddly. Perhaps she has never quite come to terms with her own ambition. Given her self-confessed superstition and 'glass half-empty' personality, ambition is something that she is clearly not comfortable admitting to, either to herself or to the world. She has said, too, that she had no grand plan to take on the most successful comedians of the time, the Jo Brands and the Mark Thomases of the stand-up circuit, and beat them at their own game.

'I didn't ever set out to conquer the stand-up world. It was just a happy coincidence that I loved doing it and it seemed to take off. But what it absolutely did was that it led me to Edinburgh – and Edinburgh is a big trade fair, basically.'

She means, of course, the annual Edinburgh Festival that takes place every August in the Scottish capital. An institution since 1947, the Edinburgh Festival comprises a range of official and unofficial performances encompassing not only comedy but music, theatre, dance and film. Given a great deal of attention by the national press, it's a sure-fire forum for gaining recognition. For comedians, the biggest deal has always been the Perrier Awards, now the If Comedy Awards. Previous winners of this award have usually gone on to greater things and the illustrious list includes Sean Hughes, Frank Skinner, Steve Coogan, Lee Evans, Dylan Moran and the League Of Gentlemen. Even to get nominated for the award guarantees a high profile.

It was as part of fellow stand-up comedian Lee Mack's show *New Bits* at the Edinburgh Festival that she first drew the attention of audiences and critics. Mack, now famous for starring in the BBC sitcom *Not Going Out* is a comedian who has had a high-profile stand-up career and his own show on Radio 2,

The Lee Mack Show. His *New Bits* show was a series of sketches interspersed with video footage that also starred Tate and fellow stand-up Dan Antopolski.

As part of this ensemble show in 2000, she was nominated for a Perrier award and thus discussed within the pages of virtually every broadsheet paper in the land. For Lee Mack, who had worked with Tate over the years on the comedy circuit, she was an obvious choice to join him on stage, but he also proved her very astute understanding that being in Edinburgh would lead her to where she wanted to go.

Said Mack: 'I first saw Catherine doing a five-minute stand-up spot in a new act competition. It was clear she was very, very good and was going to be very successful. If I'm going to be honest though, and this isn't a joke, I asked her to be in my show because not only did I think she was very talented, but also I knew she was going to be at Edinburgh anyway, so I wouldn't have to pay for her accommodation.'

It's amazing that it is something as simple as this which can make or break a career. Had Tate not already worked out that being in Edinburgh was of paramount importance in getting further up the career ladder, and so booked her own humble digs, she might never have been part of Lee Mack's *New Bits*. And if she had never been part of Lee Mack's *New Bits,* then she might never have been nominated for a Perrier, garnered positive critical attention and been able to return to Edinburgh the following year with her own fully-fledged one-woman show.

Let's remember also that this was not a full-time occupation that paid the bills. Rather her performance was something she had to labour over in the evenings and at weekends after her full-time job as receptionist for an American pensions company.

Of course she needed talent to succeed. But she also needed to put in long hours for years on top of a day job to ever get where she is today. Yet this is a period she looks back on with great fondness, and with perhaps even a misty-eyed nostalgia: 'It is more exciting when there is everything to play for than when you're in the game. Things start to go right and you become less happy.'

If that's a truthful statement rather than one of her self-deprecating jokes, then it's a pretty sad state of affairs. But more of her battle with her negative demons later.

*

Those relatively few punters who saw Catherine Tate in *New Bits* would have witnessed the development of Nan, along with terrifying teen Lauren and camp as Christmas Derek, one of the three most popular characters in Tate's future BBC sketch show. The old lady, who first came over as sweet then suffered sudden mood swings to change into a blaspheming old bag, was an instant hit.

Developed in Tate's years of stand-up spots, Nan was given a prominent role in *New Bits*. On television, Nan would be aided by expensive prosthetics and make-up. On stage, however, Tate merely donned a headscarf and an old Oxfam cardigan to bring her to life – that, and the terrifying Cockney voice followed by an ear-piercing cackle, of course.

She did enough to garner this very positive review from a

Daily Telegraph critic: 'The format allowed Tate to demonstrate an extraordinary ear for mimicry, a blissfully sure sense of character and perfect comic timing. Whether she was looking on in resignation as a bored girlfriend, or cawing obscenities as an old Cockney tramp, she provided the hour's most memorable moments.'

Lee Mack must have wondered when reading this whether having Tate with him to steal the show was his wisest move. It's just as well then that he's gone onto a very successful career of his own both with sell-out stand-up tours and the popular TV sitcom *Not Going Out*.

Nan was again pressed into service for Tate's one-woman show which she played to packed houses at the Pleasance Cellar in 2001. The Pleasance is one of Edinburgh's biggest festival venues, offering 20 different theatre spaces for performance, and the Pleasance Cellar has a capacity of 50. As well as Nan, she introduced a few other prototypes that later made it to screen, as the rave reviews for her show demonstrated. Joining her on stage was Jonathan McGuinness, a talented stage actor who would later appear with Tate in her TV sketch show.

Reviewing Tate's show in *The Guardian* in August 2001, critic Brian Logan was in no doubt of her future potential. 'Suddenly, a comic acting talent blazes into view,' he wrote. 'Catherine Tate was Perrier-nominated last year as part of Lee Mack's sketch show. She now returns for her first headline show, playing five monstrous characters. The first, and weakest, is a camp old drag queen, boring his stagehand. The second is a glazed-over office girl discussing, in an absurdly protracted Essex squawk, what an 'absolute lunatic' she is. Then comes a randy nurse on the pull in the hospital waiting room ("Oh, I've got a mind like a sieve – your mother passed away"), a sozzled bride on her wedding day, and a foul-mouthed, unashamed granny. The show is packed with choice one-liners rooted in strongly conceived character – Tate's ruthless geriatric describes an ugly baby as "one eye looking at you, the other looking for you". There may not be many belly laughs here, but Tate, a former RSC actress, shows a flair for convincing transformation as she morphs through ages, accents and headgear. In sketches that will inevitably invite comparisons with Victoria Wood, Tate celebrates rather than patronises her usually dim-witted dramatis personae. In two glorious instances, her vignettes demonstrate that behind every stereotype lurks a human being with a surprise in store.'

While Tate now claims never to read her reviews, she couldn't have been anything other than over the moon with that rave from a respected broadsheet. To be compared with Victoria Wood, a comedian she had grown up idolizing, must have been a much-needed shot in the arm. And as her plan had been to travel up to Edinburgh to get some attention, it couldn't possibly have worked any better.

The respected *Edinburgh Evening News* was equally generous in its praise of Tate's performance. Experienced critic Fiona Scott-Norman awarded her one-woman show four stars and the following: 'It's good to see some decent comedy character work; it's all too rare in a festival where stand-up and sketch are king. Catherine Tate, ably assisted by Jonathan McGuinness, does perform sketches, but they're not of the zany, crazy, high-jinks kind. They are basically mini-monologues built around keenly observed, multifaceted characters. If they have anything in common, from the twenties drag queen to the manipulative grandmother, from the cynical bride to the ditzy secretary, it is a nasty streak. Tate adds spice to her characters by giving them an under- or overcurrent of meanness. The strength of this show lies in the amazing detail of Tate's observations. The writing is strong and funny enough, but the scripts would be nothing without Tate's mannerisms and vocal elasticity. She could easily have a character-based television show on the strength of these inventions, a self-centred cavalcade of women who expect the world to run on their terms.'

Here was a critic who could see the writing on the wall and, for someone who wanted to work in television, Tate couldn't have hoped for a better review. It might have taken three more years for Scott-Norman's prophecy of a television series to come true, but come true it certainly did. And we can recognize from the critics' descriptions the skeletons of not only Nan, but Bernie, the sex-mad Irish nurse, the drunken bride from the first series, and screeching, pleased-with-herself Sam from the Essex couple, Paul and Sam.

One woman who also saw the potential in Tate and her memorable yet ghastly cast of characters was casting director Tracey Gillham. Based at the BBC, Gillham is a highly experienced casting director in television and film who also cast *Jonathan Creek*, *The Office*, *Extras* and *Little Britain*. At Edinburgh to scout talent, she had caught Tate's show and afterwards sought her out with an assurance that she'd be in touch when the right project turned up.

Gillham was as good as her word and the project turned out to be *Wild West*, the BBC sitcom with Dawn French that first brought Tate to broader national attention some two years later. To be cast alongside someone as well-known and popular as French was a huge coup. As part of famous comedy duo French and Saunders, an original member of the Comic Strip and the star of *The Vicar of Dibley*, French was a household name and any project she was involved with was bound to garner huge attention.

*

In between her success in *New Bits* and her triumphant one-woman show, Tate had also been on a world tour with the RSC and met and fallen in love with her partner Twig Clark. It's no wonder that she has described this time as the happiest of her life.

Stand-up served her well over the next few years, and it was at a special showcase for then-BBC2 controller Jane Root, at the Bush Theatre in London's Shepherd Bush, that Tate finally got the nod to go ahead with *The Catherine Tate Show*.

As the first female controller of a BBC channel, Root attracted a lot of controversy during her reign from 1999 to 2004. But she also oversaw the development of cult and then mainstream hits *The Office*, *The Kumars At No.42* and *Marion And Geoff*, as well as surprise success quiz *The Weakest Link* with Anne Robinson. Her successful grooming of Catherine Tate certainly fits her track record for recognizing commercial success.

Any new material for the three series Tate devised was always tried out first in front of a live audience at anywhere from the Soho Theatre on London's Dean Street to the Latchmere, a tiny venue above a pub in south-west London. It was surely the confidence she gained from tackling live and lairy audiences that allowed her to go on and make three eponymous series for the BBC.

Anyone who caught any of her early or Edinburgh stand-up performances would realize, too, that no great changes had to be made to her characters to make them suitable for a BBC2 audience. This must have been one of the big attractions for a broadcaster looking for a brand new talent to turn into a household name: the less radical changes that have to be made, then the quicker and easier the talent can be transferred to the screen.

One man who was also mightily impressed with her stand-up talent was Arthur Mathews, co-creator with Graham Linehan of the comedy genius that was sitcom *Father Ted*. This cult comedy of the mid 1990s saw three misfit Irish priests banished to a remote isle off the west coast of Ireland along with their tea-pushing housekeeper Mrs Doyle. Tate had already acted alongside Matthews in *Big Train*, the sketch show he had co-written with Linehan, but it was only when he saw her perform her own material at the Soho Theatre a couple of years later that he realised her true potential.

'When she was on *Big Train* she was very shy and quiet,' Mathews remembered. 'She didn't have any input into the series, she just largely turned up and did the acting. She was good pals with Tracy Ann Oberman (her fellow actress who also attended Central School of Speech and Drama and played Chrissie Watts in *EastEnders*, the woman who eventually murdered Dirty Den) who is quite outgoing and she was with a lot of people there who she wouldn't have worked with before. When I went to see her in the

Soho Theatre, I realized she was very good, how character-based her stuff was and I could see then that she could do a lot more.'

He could also see how instantly commercial her act was: 'I think her natural style is very BBC1. Having seen her stage show I don't think she did anything to tailor it for television. I think that naturally what she does is very popular. I think you could compare her to *Little Britain* in a way. They're both fairly broad and commercial. It's not *The Office*, it's big performances and going in front of a live audience. I wish there was a better word than "commercial", it's whatever Ronnie Barker had... it's probably universal. I'm really pleased for her, I think she's well deserving of it.'

Mathews was asked by Tate's producer Geoffrey Perkins, who had also produced *Father Ted*, to contribute some sketches to her first series: 'I didn't work with Catherine directly – what happened was that I just sent her lots of sketches.' His contributions included the Enigmatic Cop who talked nonsense to her puzzled sidekick and sang Pretenders' lyrics, and the woman in the very first episode who tells her date that she's 'just not drunk enough' to find him attractive.

As Tate got into her stride with the show, so his contributions dwindled: 'I think what happens really with people is that if it's their own show, they'll start off using lots of writers but then as they get more confident, they'll write more of it themselves. I think that's what happened with that.'

*

Debate has raged for years as to whether women can be funny, particularly when they're generating their own material. While the Victoria Woods and Jo Brands of this world should have put paid to this years ago, there is still the odd misogynistic rumble. Given Victoria Wood's sterling track record in one-woman television shows as well as sitcom *Dinnerladies*, Brand being described as a 'national treasure' by none other than Michael Parkinson and French and Saunders continuing comic storming of national television, there really is little evidence for these theories though.

Arthur Mathews doesn't see Tate's humour as being gender-specific though. 'It's not particularly female is it? I'd say it's ballsy. She does that man, of course, although he's kind of gay isn't he?' Kind of gay? Derek Faye with the gentleman's sponge bag? Mathews laughs: 'OK, yes, he's very gay.'

When asked about the relative rarity of female stand-up comedians, Tate was fairly quick to dismiss the idea of it being any harder on the circuit as a woman. 'I do think audiences judge you perhaps a bit quicker if you're a woman, but I don't think you should be put off it. You have to have a bit of a male attitude towards it because women are more sensitive and if you do get a succession of rough gigs it does take a lot to go, "I am going to carry on doing this, they are not going to get me down." Though you do need to be very clear that if you are dying on your arse it may be just because you're not that good at it. To be honest, I think there's a little bit of pussyfooting around when people make excuses for women or women make excuses for themselves because, whether you're male or female, if you're not funny, you're not funny. I don't think making people laugh is a particularly gender-specific thing.'

One of those periodic surveys that seem to be done only to fill up the pages of newspapers was published in 2006 in a scientific journal: *Evolution and Human Behaviour*. Its premise was that men don't fancy funny women. Lead researcher on the survey Doctor Rod Martin was quoted as saying: 'When they're forced to choose between humour appreciation and humour production in potential partners, women valued humour production, while men valued appreciation of their own humour. One reason men don't like female comedians may be that humour is seen as a masculine thing.'

Catherine Tate was swift and categorical with her response. 'I recognize this type of man. They think if you are being funny, then you are entering their domain. They're the kind of man who assumes a woman cracking a joke is a lesbian. It's mad. After all I wouldn't be threatened by a man who could cook would I?' Given that she told celebrity magazine *Heat* that she'd never cooked a 'proper' dinner in her life, and that a meal round at hers was likely to consist of a bowl of cereal followed by a Penguin biscuit, it's probably just as well.

Jokes about comedy aside, Tate has analysed her humour and appeal when pressed. She told *The Times*: 'Comedy has to be eight parts recognition, one part shock, and one part exaggeration. I suppose, whereas *Little Britain* was a snapshot of the country, my show is a snapshot of women's lives. The only device we have is me...'

Little Britain crops up a lot in the same breath as *The Catherine Tate Show*. Both comedy sketch shows, they aired at roughly the same time. Created by Matt Lucas and David Walliams, *Little Britain* showcased grotesque characters that also dominated the public imagination. Most popular was Vicky Pollard who has been compared endlessly to Tate's Lauren. This shell-suited, mouthy schoolgirl popularized the 'Yeah, but no, but yeah' catchphrase and became a bête noire along with Lauren for those trying to pin blame for the breakdown of teenage behaviour. Both stroppy teenagers, their meeting has been mooted and would surely be a match made at the bus stop outside the precinct. Said Tate of a Vicki/ Lauren encounter: 'It has been talked about. Maybe for something like *Comic Relief*. Wouldn't it be great to have them meet down at the ASBO office and find out they were stepsisters!'

She is aware, too, that she is not a writer of gags, and is more an observer of human nature at its most extreme. She described her show thus: 'There are long character-driven sketches, which often don't end on gags. There are no "gag" gags in my show. I like to let the characters breathe a bit, and some can hold their own in terms of length. Like Nan. She's got a lot to say.'

Some of her sketches have been criticised for being overly long, a common complaint about all shows of this nature. Anyone sitting through another, seemingly endless riff between Essex couple Paul and Sam could probably see the validity of this particular criticism. But no-one has a perfect strike rate, and Tate can be forgiven the odd overlong sketch given the belly laughs provided by her more winning creations.

As self-critical and self-deprecating as ever, she says she wouldn't even claim to be a 'proper' writer. 'Maybe it's just me being shy, but I think a real writer writes for everyone, whereas at the moment I just write for myself. I'm interested in the way people speak. I don't write gags; I wouldn't know how to. My comedy isn't about saying funny things, it's about saying things funny.'

She does admit that comedy is 'in her bones', however, and that she doesn't think she'd ever be able to stay away from it for too long. It's sad that an often talked-about live national tour of *The Catherine Tate Show* never materialized; the *Little Britain* one was a smash hit and hers would surely have been too.

As good as Tate is at live comedy, and as addictive as she obviously finds it, let's hope that she hasn't abandoned the idea of a face-to-face audience for comedy altogether.

CHAPTER FOUR

Television Break

Having been spotted by casting agent Tracey Gillham while performing her sell-out one woman show at Edinburgh's Pleasance Cellar, it wasn't long before Catherine Tate got the phone call that would change her life.

Gillham wanted her to audition for the part of Angela in a brand new sitcom by veteran writer Simon Nye. Having already created *Is It Legal?*, *How Do You Want Me?* and the award-winning *Men Behaving Badly*, the sitcom that gave lager louts a slightly better name, Nye's attachment to the project already meant a certain cachet. That her co-star would be Dawn French, one of Tate's comedy heroines, must have sent her mind racing with the possibilities this project offered.

The show was *Wild West* and the producers and French were looking for someone who could gel with this established star and hold her own against such a recognizable and larger than life character.

On meeting Tate, French was immediately impressed: 'I'd never met Catherine Tate until she came to the audition, but she's such an unusual and interesting talent I was completely drawn to her straight away. I don't think I've ever met anyone quite like her – she is genuinely barking. But in a very clever way. In fact, she was a bit too talented for my liking and may have to be destroyed.'

Given her lengthy and successful partnership with Jennifer Saunders, French needed someone to play off who could replace her veteran partner almost seamlessly. The chemistry with Tate seemed to work from the very beginning. 'I knew that part had to be played by someone I really wanted to work with. I'm so used to Jennifer that you get a bit lazy really. There's so much I don't have to say to Jen and we are very good at taking each other's temperatures if things might get heated. Maybe it's a female thing, or maybe we're both just too lazy to ever have a row. I didn't want to be working with a person where you just have to constantly explain everything or where they can't improvise a little bit with you. Luckily Catherine was really good at that and we had a hoot.'

French's character in *Wild West* was Mary Trewednack, a village postmistress in a Cornish coastal hamlet. Tate played Angela, her partner both in the local shop and in life. The pair were lesbian lovers, but really only because no-one else would have them. The comedy involved the local goings-on, with other important characters being the landlord and landlady of the local pub, the woman who ran the local witchcraft centre, and an elderly fisherman.

While it has been compared to *The Vicar of Dibley*, French's other very successful sitcom, in that they both had rural settings and an oddball range of 'local' characters, *Wild West* had a darker edge with plots involving sexual swinging, menacing youths and other weirdness. It could probably be best described as the quirkiness of *Ballykissangel* meets the out and out craziness of *The League of Gentlemen* set in Cornwall.

Written especially for French by Nye, it was designed to help her shrug off any typecasting that had come with *The Vicar of Dibley*. Said French: 'From the minute I started to play Geraldine Granger [the Vicar of Dibley] it has been very hard to shake her off. Not that I really want to shake her off – I'm very fond of her – but I need to be able to play different roles. The feel of *Wild West* is also very unlike *Dibley* as it hasn't got all that bright squeaky cleanliness. It's not all shot through lovely filters making everything look sunny. Quite the opposite, in fact – the village and the people who live there are quite dark and a little bit sinister. But that's what attracted me to it.'

Already pregnant with daughter Erin when filming began, Tate was now faced with two simultaneous life-changing events. This was fairly overwhelming as was obvious from an interview after the shooting had finished: 'If you had told me a year ago that I would be starring opposite Dawn French, I wouldn't have believed you; and if you had told me I would be expecting a baby I wouldn't have believed you either. But landing my biggest job and having a baby at the same time has meant that my life has not been dominated by either one.'

It seems that Tate got over any star struck behaviour around her heroine fairly early on, no matter how impressed she was: 'I couldn't believe my luck getting to work with Dawn French – I'm

a huge admirer. Dawn and I stayed in the same hotel in a tiny
village in Cornwall. We were filming in summer 2002 and my
abiding memory is of *Big Brother 3*. Dawn and I were massive
fans. We used to get the man in the village to video it for us when
we were shooting night scenes. Dawn loved Adele and I liked Jade
Goody.' One of the most notorious series of the reality television
show, *Big Brother 3* was famous for introducing the world to
Jade Goody. Her comical geographical misunderstandings and
drunken behaviour made her both a tabloid scapegoat and,
conversely, one of the most popular housemates. Her career flour-
ished until she entered *Celebrity Big Brother* in 2007 and became
involved in an allegedly racist row with Bollywood star Shilpa
Shetty. Accusations of bullying were also made.

It sounds like they had a fine old time watching Jade expose
her 'kebab'(her belly though it was suggested she meant somewhere more intimate) and trying to figure out whether fellow
contestant PJ had indeed received sexual favours from Jade under
the duvet. The fact that they got on so well was a tremendous
relief for Tate who was familiar with that old adage 'never meet
your heroes': 'She's just very, very unstarry and very funny in a
way that lifts your heart, because French and Saunders had been
real heroes of mine, and there's part of you that thinks: "What are
they going to be like?"'

While *Wild West* failed to set the world alight, Tate was excellent as Angela, the more sensible sidekick of the frankly bonkers
Mary Trewednack. Again, part of the attraction of the project for
French was Mary's dissimilarity to Geraldine, her *Vicar of Dibley*
alter ego. 'Mary's very unusual and I suppose she is the opposite

of the vicar. She's quite alarming because she says what she thinks, usually without considering the sensitivity of the situation. She just blurts out whatever is on her mind, which gets her into a lot of trouble. Mary's also borderline violent, so you wouldn't want to have an argument with her. She likes to get her own way. Sometimes her rows with Angela escalate into quite a lot of physical violence which I really enjoyed doing. I do like being paid to punch people – it's very fulfilling.'

Given French's already high profile and the larger than life nature of Mary, Tate had quite a challenge to step up and match her. But she does so effortlessly and commands as much attention from the viewer as if she'd been doing this for years.

Angela is also an interesting role as we slowly discover that the character has a history of mental breakdowns, is prone to panic attacks and has phobias about many things including the dark. She's in denial about the panic attacks, though, repeatedly claiming 'there was a bear outside the window' when challenged about her meltdowns.

Tate somehow manages to make this bundle of neuroses very funny and, if you lasted throughout the whole two series, Angela is a character you grow fond of, despite her general terror of life. It was also a good job that Angela was a naturally scruffy character, as the wardrobe department had no problems hiding Tate's growing baby bump under a hideous mass of elasticated waist skirts, big baggy jumpers and cagoules.

The lesbianism felt like a bit of tokenism. While you saw the pair in bed together, there was no actual physical affection. It was definitely more Morecambe and Wise in striped pyjamas than hot girl on girl action. And any time a half-decent man hove into view, the pair would end up fighting over him.

As a positive portrayal of one type of sexual choice, it left a lot to be desired. As French said: 'Simon Nye has no doubt that Mary and Angela are lesbians but they're also open to whatever comes their way. They're just randy. When an eligible man arrives, they fight over him. I'm always on for a big old gay snog but there's none of that here. I can promise you won't see any big hot lesbo action going on. This isn't *Tipping The Velvet*.' French was referring to a novel with lesbian content by Sarah Waters which was turned into a popular BBC drama series with many talked about scenes of women becoming intimate with each other.

In fact, by the time the second series rolled around, it had been decided to put the lesbianism to bed, so to speak. The first episode of the second series saw Mary and Angela snogging half-heartedly and deciding they were over the whole lesbian thing. So they both set out to find a boyfriend by drawing up a list of potentials and sticking it to the wall.

Apparently, the series had been tested among focus groups of viewers and French's fan base were none too keen on the Sapphic angle. As Tate explained prior to the second series: 'It seems the focus groups didn't like the idea of Dawn, well... it was all a bit too scary... two ladies in bed...'

French as Mary thus developed a long-running relationship with the local policeman, while Angela took up with a selfish hitchhiker she'd picked up locally. For viewers who liked their comedies on the cosy side, heterosexuality was a much safer option.

While *Wild West* had its fans, they didn't blossom in great numbers and viewing figures fell steadily throughout the second series. The television critics didn't exactly rave about it either, though it did win some over. Jaci Stephen, writing in *The Mail On Sunday* described it as 'Mad, mad, mad and so funny'.

Sam Wollaston in *The Guardian* tried to like the second series but failed, concluding: 'I wanted to like this one. It does more than just gags; it tries to be a little bit kooky; there's a touch of the dark side, too. But I didn't laugh – it wasn't funny last time they tried it, and it isn't funny now. And that's a problem for a sitcom.'

The highly acerbic Victor Lewis-Smith of the *Evening Standard* took an altogether stronger view, feeling that it patronised those that lived in the countryside to an unpalatable degree. Never one to mince his words he wrote: 'Farm animals have been Disneyfied for decades by television and now the people who inhabit the British countryside are being Dibleyfied. First came the detestable *Vicar of Dibley*, portraying country dwellers as harmless simpletons for the amusement of sophisticated city folk, and now we've had BBC1's *Wild West* depicting them as nothing more than a bunch of parochial inbred cretins, and dishonest cretins at that.'

He didn't end there either, clearly passionate about defending the Cornish people from lazy stereotype: 'As if Cornwall hasn't had enough to put up with in recent years, what with Oxfordshire-raised Rick Stein and his cod Padstow accent patronisingly adopting the locals and their ancient culture, it's now been thoroughly traduced over the past six weeks by the usually surefooted Simon Nye. He recently admitted that he'd never even visited the county before penning his condescending and humour-free sitcom, and the only purpose it's served has been to reinforce the prejudices of certain metropolitan media types that rural existence is inherently worthless and absurd, and that city life is the only life worth living.'

Despite a critical mauling and less than stunning viewing figures *Wild West* certainly did Tate's career no harm. It brought someone unknown outside the tiny circles of theatre and stand-up comedy into the nation's living rooms. The association with comedy superstar French also served her well, particularly given French's much-quoted line about her being too talented and having to be destroyed. Shortly after finishing filming in the Cornish village of Portloe, Tate was offered the first series of *The Catherine Tate Show* and she was thus immediately able to capitalize on her heightened profile.

*

Of course, as we've already seen, Tate had done television before but her appearances were usually of the 'blink and you'd miss them' variety. After bit parts in long-running dramas like *The Bill*, her comedy then allowed her to work on a variety of sketch shows. These were often incredibly different to her natural style, which at least shows her versatility.

One of these was *Attention Scum*, a six-part series that was shown late at night on BBC2 in 2001. Fronted by comedian Simon Munnery posing as 'The League Against Tedium', it was a heightened and surrealist comedy which also featured Johnny Vegas and Kevin Eldon. Tate appeared in a variety of sketches but the show was given a graveyard slot and sank without trace.

In the same year, she popped up in *TV Go Home*, another six-part sketch show, this time for E4. Developed from a website that spoofed the *Radio Times*, this too didn't make a great impact on viewers and also only ran to one series.

Big Train, the BBC sketch show from the *Father Ted* writers was more successful but not hugely so. Tate was cast in this because of her ability to speak French, and she appeared in one sketch in which she broke up with her French lover in favour of going out with a traffic light. Writer Arthur Mathews thought Tate excellent in this crazy role.

She also developed some of her own sketch material in Channel 4's *Barking*, a show that also gave career opportunities to Mackenzie Crook (later to star in *The Office*), Peter Kay and David Walliams. The producers thought that an early prototype of the Lauren character, a mouthy streetwise teen, too cutting edge and those sketches were never aired. Performances in both *The Harry Hill Show* and *That Peter Kay Thing* followed and won her new friends and fans. All this groundwork meant that, when her big break eventually came, she was more than ready for it.

Her choice of television work since *The Catherine Tate Show* took off has been interesting, not least because there's not much of it. It can't have been too difficult a decision to appear as Mrs Chadband in the BBC's adaptation of Charles Dickens' *Bleak House* in 2005. The stern minister's wife was obviously a big break from her comedy characters and a chance to prove her serious acting skills. Critically acclaimed, the production also starred actors of the calibre of Gillian Anderson, Charles Dance, Timothy West and Alun Armstrong.

She also appeared in *Marple: A Murder Is Announced* as Mitzi Kosinski, a Jewish refugee, alongside the very grand Geraldine McEwan playing Agatha Christie's detective Miss Marple. The cast lists for these occasional ITV Marple adaptations read like a *Who's Who* of veteran British acting talent, so that was a smart choice on Tate's part.

Another smart choice was her lead role in *The Bad Mother's Handbook*, a one-off ITV drama adapted by Kate Long, the author of the best-selling book of the same name. As Tate explained at the time: 'The misconception about the book is that it's labelling someone a bad mum. It's actually about the fictional handbook we are all handed when we become mothers and how we can get it wrong.'

In *The Bad Mother's Handbook*, Tate plays Karen, a northern mum of a teenager and the daughter of a woman who is beginning to suffer from dementia. The latter character is played by Anne Reid and Tate explained her involvement thus: 'I just loved the book and then I heard Anne Reid was going to play my mum. She's a real heroine of mine so it was a done deal after that.'

Reid first became famous as Valerie Tatlock in *Coronation Street*, a role she played for ten years until 1971. A varied career included her playing Jean in Victoria Wood's *Dinnerladies* and a BAFTA nomination for Best Actress In A Leading Role in 2004 for *The Mother*. Much loved and respected, Reid is an actress that younger performers tend to look up to and playing with her would be a great honour.

Although *The Bad Mother's Handbook* is a comedy-drama, Karen is a deeply miserable character who feels she has been short-changed by life. It is only towards the very end of the ninety-minute piece that we get to see a softer side of Karen. It seems that Tate, now used to being in charge of her own series, couldn't resist adding a few suggestions of her own.

Kate Long, writing a piece in the *Daily Mail Weekend* magazine about being on set, describes Tate's input thus: 'Catherine came in with suggestions – (she) wanted to see more of Karen's boss Leo (Steve Pemberton). Likes him, can he provide more of a romantic interest? She's convinced her character would find facial hair a turn-off and adds a line to say so.'

While Tate's comic judgement and writing talent is well-established, it must be hard for another writer like Kate Long to take on board 'suggestions' from an actress who is also a writer. This, then, is the dilemma that faces Tate as she forges ahead with her career. Does she allow her inner control freak to take charge and only do projects where she can be in total control? Or does she relinquish some of the responsibility and become attached to things where she can't sway the outcome of the finished product?

As is true in so much of life, a fine balance between the two would probably make for a more satisfying career and be the most sensible option.

CHAPTER FIVE

The Catherine Tate Show

Towards the end of 2002, Catherine Tate had finished filming on her new BBC sitcom with her comedy heroine Dawn French and was heavily pregnant with daughter Erin. The BBC had already expressed some interest in developing her own sketch show, but nothing had been confirmed.

She was asked to try out some material for the then BBC2 supremo Jane Root at the Bush Theatre in West London. An intimate theatre above the Bush pub on Shepherds Bush Green, the Bush is a stone's throw from BBC TV Centre and popular with BBC staff. It has had a reputation for championing new writing since the early 1970s. As Tate recalled afterwards: 'We did a forty-minute show at the Bush Theatre for Jane Root to see it, and I was eight months pregnant at the time. Frankly, I just wanted to sit down.'

Her tiredness must not have come across because shortly afterwards Tate was offered that holy grail for any aspiring comedy writer: her very own series.

In February 2003, some six months after giving birth to Erin, she started work on what would be her first six-part series, the first episode of which went out on February 16, 2004. Plagued by postnatal depression, she nonetheless battled through to produce something that would delight both critics and an audience crying out for comedy characters they could relate to.

However, she admitted later that she really didn't think The *Catherine Tate Show* would be a hit, or that her catchphrases would become national currency: 'It's nuts. When you see "bovvered" going into the Oxford English Dictionary, or used in headlines, or hear it around you – you go, "Oh, it's not just me and my immediate circle of friends." It's really, really weird and really, really amazing. I'm also a bit detached from it.'

She hooked up with legendary television comedy producer Geoffrey Perkins to make the series, a man associated with ground-breaking puppet satire show *Spitting Image* and *Father Ted* as well as Ben Elton and Harry Enfield. Both Elton and Enfield had started their careers on the stand-up comedy circuit and went on to become national figures through their own television shows. Perkins has a fantastic track record for developing comedy talent and his faith in Tate, and guidance, would be invaluable.

They proved a great team, as he seemed to understand instinctively her character-based comedy. In fact it was Perkins who persuaded her that she should develop Lauren for the show, a move she was reluctant to make.

The now legendary schoolgirl was first dreamt up by Tate for a Channel 4 sketch show called *Barking* but the producers of that decided she was a little too edgy for their tastes. 'We shot the sketches and they didn't use them – they said we're a bit worried it's a bit too edgy, and I thought, "Gosh, is it?" – and then about six months later Ali G came out.'

Ali G was a fictional character developed by Sacha Baron Cohen who made his debut on *The Eleven O'Clock Show* on Channel 4. A white, middle-class suburban male from Staines masquerading as a street-wise 'gangsta' – he specialized in outrageous interviews in which he fooled celebrities and politicians into believing he was black and the 'voice of da yoof'. He went on to have his own show, also on Channel 4, *Da Ali G Show* and had catchphrases such as 'Booyakasha', 'Big Up Yaself', 'Respek' and 'Is it cos I is black?' The similarities between Ali G and Lauren aren't enormous, but they were both streetwise characters with big mouths and no respect for authority.

'I hesitated before using the character in my new show, because I think that Ali G thing's been done now, but my producer, Geoffrey Perkins, persuaded me it was different. I'm pleased we did because it's been the one which has got the most interest.'

When developing the show, Tate tried out new characters and material at the tiny Latchmere Theatre in south-west London. Yet another theatre above a pub, this seats only a few dozen people and not in great comfort. The phrase 'am I bovvered?' was only in the sketch two or three times but it raised such a laugh each time that she decided to keep saying it. And every time she did, the louder the laughter became.

Over the years, she seems to have developed a bit of a love/hate relationship with one of her most famous characters, but at least she was a breeze to do in terms of make-up and costume.

'Luckily Lauren is one of the easiest characters to do. There's no real make-up: I just scrape my hair up and put on a bit of mascara. If she was covered in foundation, she'd look too grown up.'

She explains that the character developed from observing a host of teenage girls and their attitudes: 'Teenagers today are just so louche. And so defensive. You say something simple like "Hello" and Lauren would immediately say, "Are you calling me a thief? Are you?" But it's not meant to be derogatory. More of a comment that girls like this are everywhere.'

An instant hit and widely copied in schools and offices around the country, Lauren and her truculent catchphrases were soon more famous than her creator. But Lauren's lengthy monologues were difficult to learn and Tate ended up not loving her as much as the rest of the nation did: 'To be honest, I'm not as attached to Lauren as everyone else is. Learning her lines is quite tricky because I have to come in really quickly with a long rant.'

One of the trickiest to perform was one where Lauren is attempting a French oral exam. Having sent her French teacher to the brink of distraction, she then launches into fluent French, with the word 'bovvered' inserted at appropriate moments. 'The French exam sketch was good fun to do, but the Lauren stuff is less enjoyable than the others because it's such a technical performance. That said, I do love her because I know the audience loves her.'

This love wasn't enough to stop Tate killing off the girl with the inventive line in backchat though. In the 2007 Christmas special of *The Catherine Tate Show*, Lauren uttered her very last 'bovvered?' before disappearing over a Dorset waterfall on a school kayaking trip.

As she donned an orange life jacket and had her hair scraped back for the final time to live out Lauren's last moments, Tate was unrepentant. 'I'm not sad at all,' she said, 'If we ever did a live show, of course she'd be resurrected. She'd be sitting on top of a cloud. There's just nowhere else for her to go.'

She had felt this ever since the famous *Comic Relief* sketch when Lauren went to Number Ten Downing Street as a work experience girl, causing then Prime Minister Tony Blair to launch into his own 'Face? Bovvered?' routine. The BBC annual *Comic Relief* marathon raises money for charities and has always featured high profile sketches and celebrity appearances. But Tate's visit to Number Ten and Blair's ready involvement, throwing himself into Lauren's routine with abandon, attracted a huge amount of publicity.

'I just didn't know how to top the Prime Minister sketch. You can't just go, "Christmas pudding, am I bovvered?", can you? I'm delighted the way the whole thing's gone, but I've got to move on. If I just keep dressing as a schoolgirl, saying, "Am I bovvered?", I can't blame people for thinking that's all I do.'

As well as a possible post-mortem appearance at a future live show, she hasn't entirely ruled out a Bobby Ewing *Dallas*-style resurrection of Lauren either: 'I just want to say that no-one has recovered a body! There's always room for her to step back out of a shower two years down the line.'

*

While Tate has come up with more than forty original comic creations, it is probably Nan who is the next best known after Lauren. This cantankerous old lady was developed from a character she used to great effect in her stand-up comedy shows, something which makes her unique.

'None of my other characters started when I did stand-up, but I used to do a story about my nan – she's not like my nan at all, but you say that on stage – and that voice just came out. It was part of the stand-up I knew would always go well. I'd think, I've got the old bag, bring her on.'

The old bag proved to be comedy gold, once fleshed out creepily and crêpe-like by an expert team of make-up and prosthetic artists. Prosthetics expert Neill Gorton and make-up designer Vanessa White collaborated on bringing the monstrous old lady to life. As Gorton explains: 'In the case of Nan, Vanessa had this fantastic picture of Bette Davis when she was older. It wasn't that we were trying to make Nan look like Bette Davis, it was more the hair that defined her. Nan has this great, roots-growing-out-don't-give-a-damn hairstyle that really nails her character. If she had a grey bun or a blue rinse it wouldn't work.'

This was all a bit of a shock for Tate, who, when she played Nan on stage, was used to simply donning a headscarf and putting on the voice. 'I wore a headscarf and a charity shop cardigan and that was it. Now, when I do Nan for the show, I have £1,500 prosthetics on my face.' She was delighted with the professionalism of the work done though: 'It's the neck, and you can see it more when I swallow.'

Despite, or maybe because of the lengthy transformation, she has said that Nan is her favourite character to play: 'It's the one character I can look at on screen and not find myself in. It's a very good transformation. In lots of the others it's clear that it's me. I just enjoy playing that character mainly because you get the privilege of age where you can swear and people laugh. Old people swearing is funny.'

She is pleased, too, that lots of people tell her that they know someone just like Nan and says that she based her on an amalgam of old ladies from her local community in Bloomsbury. However, she was also slightly worried that some confused audience members might think she was an actual person: 'Some people must think she's real. I was recognized in the supermarket the other day, and the woman said, "Ooh, you look a lot younger in real life, dear."'

*

If there was ever a third contender to join the holy trinity of top Catherine Tate creations, then it would have to be Derek Faye, the outrageously camp, yet in the closet, mincer. This is probably the most startling physical transformation for Tate, and the only male character she plays herself. On his first 'outing', she found herself getting entirely confused as to her own gender when she had to use a pub toilet.

'I suddenly thought, "God, I look like a man, so which toilet do I go in?" I went into the women's but then started ridiculously explaining myself, as one lady was a bit freaked out.'

Derek is also the biggest challenge for the production team, given his antithetical appearance to Tate's own. As Neill Gorton explains: 'With him you have the opposite of Catherine in both gender and hair. Catherine is female with masses of hair, Derek is male and bald. It's also the case that Vanessa loves bald characters and I'm good at making bald characters, so bald was where we went with it.'

Derek is also the character that takes the longest to do. 'When we first did Derek I think it was four hours. It takes half an hour just to flatten and wrap her hair because there's so much of it. For series three I had the luxury of redesigning Derek's make-up to speed up the process, and we're now down to two and a half hours.'

*

Given the horrific appearance of both Nan and Derek, it's obvious that Tate lacks vanity and is fearless when it comes to looking grotesque – both essential qualities for a character comedy actress. She appears well aware of this, telling *The Guardian*: 'Apart from *Friends*, comedy is rarely glamorous. You've got to compromise your dignity in some way for it to work and what's nice about grotesque characters is that they display a lack of vanity. I think women now are not frightened to appear unattractive... Characters work best when they're a mixture of recognition and exaggeration and the funnier you can look within the realms of naturalism, the better. It's through the mouths of these grotesques that you can get away with things you couldn't otherwise.'

This is certainly true of Nan whose effing and blinding is legendary and who's not averse to the odd spot of out and out racism and homophobia, yet somehow manages not to offend the majority of viewers. As Tate explained: 'I do a character of an old woman who says things that, on a script in black and white, would be unacceptable. That these characters don't believe they're wrong is what makes it funny while taking the edge off the offence.'

One of the questions she has most been asked over her few years in the limelight is where she gets her characters from. On a tolerant day, she'll say from the community in which she grew up. When she's feeling more mischievous, she's been known to say, with a totally straight face: 'As has been widely documented, I get my characters from Felix Pike and Son in Drury Lane – characters by the yard.'

As incredible as this sounds, some people have taken this at face value. If you were thinking of taking a Catherine Tate field trip to London, don't bother trawling Drury Lane in Covent Garden for such an establishment as it doesn't exist. It is spitting distance from the primary school she attended, however, which is what must have given her the idea in the first place.

While obviously not wishing to make any great artistic claims about her comedy work, or to appear luvvie-like, she is proud of the characters she has created. She told the *Radio Times*: 'I don't want to say my work is based on truth – it's only a sketch show, for God's sake. But it kind of is. Otherwise, what is the point?'

Indeed, and it is in the recognition and identification with even the most embarrassing characters that the comedy lies. There is a definite audience affection for these dysfunctional people too, as, without that, the show certainly could not have gone on to three series. Tate's own affection for her characters also shines through in some of her descriptions. If she didn't feel it, then there would be no hope of us feeling it either.

While Essex couple Paul and Sam may not be people you'd want to spend any of your quality leisure time with, there is something that we warm to about the pair who crack each other up. As Tate explains: 'They were loosely based on people I know, or things that people I know would do, like make quite a banal story into the highlight of the day. They're sort of joyous characters for that reason. Wouldn't it be great to be them? It really wouldn't take much to ensure you had a good day. To find someone who loves you as much as you love yourself...'

Even closer to home were the paranoid New Parents who refuse to do anything that might wake their baby up – even forcing their friends and hosts to bring their lovingly prepared Jamie Oliver salmon dauphinoise out to them in their car in the driveway. Tate was herself a brand new parent when she was crafting the show, and admits that this was drawn directly from her own experiences. 'That's me. That was me. Sleep becomes like a commodity, a currency that goes up the less you get it. I think it is a bit of a specific thing for people who've got children.'

She's clearly very fond of Bernie, the over-sexed, over-affectionate and, frankly, completely useless nurse. When asked who would be Bernie's ideal man, she doesn't hesitate before naming the ex-*Baywatch* hunk. 'I'd say David Hasselhoff features quite highly. His ruggedness, and he looks like he'd give you a good ride. There's not many she'd turn her nose up at I don't think.'

Elaine Figgis, the Leeds bakery worker who weds a cannibalistic Death Row inmate, also makes her smile instantly. 'I love Elaine. I think to her there are worse things than killing a few people and tasting them. In your youth.'

The How Much/ How Many woman who drives her office colleague insane by forcing her to guess everything is also loosely based on herself: 'I do that quite a lot. Guess! I like guessing games. And she's naturally quite menacing. As am I.'

Margaret, the woman who screams at the tiniest provocation was inspired by her mum, Josephine: 'God, it used to embarrass me the way she yelped if someone so much as tapped her on the shoulder.'

The Aga Saga woman, who feels like her life is about to end when confronted with a gooseberry and cinnamon yoghurt past its sell-by date, came from shopping trips on London's posh Kings Road: 'Peter Jones [the department store] on the Kings Road is rife with these kind of people who genuinely seem to have nothing better to do than fret about olives.'

John Leary's mum, the harder-than-nails Northern Irish woman, who reacts surprisingly well to the news that her son is gay, also came directly from experience. 'It's a true story. A gay friend of mine from Northern Ireland was a bit worried about telling his mum he was gay – but she was so delighted about it, it embarrassed him more. He was sitting with his mates and his mum comes in and points to pictures of men in magazines and goes, "Oh, John. D'ya like him? Ooh, he's nice."'

A charity worker knocking on her door gave birth to Geordie Georgie, the star of the third series, whose endless appeals for ridiculous causes drove her co-worker to distraction and almost certain financial ruin. 'A woman wearing a Tibetan hat… knocked at my door and clearly thought I was not giving as much as she thought I should.' Whether the hapless charity mugger has seen her alter-ego on screen will probably never be known.

Other characters such as Laura Powers the rubbish spy and Ma Willow came directly from Tate's love of television. She confesses to being a massive fan of 24, the cultishly popular American drama series that follows the actions in real time of an American agent trying to foil terrorist plots. She describes it as 'Genuine, white knuckle viewing! Watching it is like taking heroin. Not that I ever have… I play British agent Laura Powers who thinks she can save the world but, as you can see, she's not very good at it.' This hapless, fumbling woman who can't even work a computer is a far cry from the fearless Jack Bauer played so brilliantly by Kiefer Sutherland. There's little likelihood that Jack would cause a bomb to go off because he didn't press 'send' on his email in time.

Her love of the hugely popular time travel drama *Life On Mars* also gave her the perfect opportunity to play around with the 1950s. While *Mars* had recreated the 1970s in Manchester through the conceit of a cop in a coma who had woken up 35 years in the past, she wanted to try a different decade and in a comedic context. 'I always wanted to do a 1950s character, but we needed a context. The detective drama *Life On Mars* gave us a fantastic premise and *Life At Ma's* is a homage. It allows Ma Willow to say all the things they said in the '50slike not being able to believe that someone doesn't smoke.'

The *Life At Ma's* sketches in the Christmas special also allowed her to invite along special guest Philip Glenister, who played Gene Hunt in the original series. His portrayal of the swaggering, politically incorrect, side-burn sporting Gene had been the highlight of the two series, winning him many female fans and critical acclaim. Glenister seemed delighted to be asked along for the ride, and played a 1950s seaside plod who ends up arresting Tate's version of the time-travelling cop for wearing too tight trunks. A glittering array of other guests have also queued up to join the Tate hi-jinks. The most high profile was probably global superstar and former Wham! singer George Michael, who proved what a good sport he was by playing a hospital patient who ends up being snogged by sex-mad Bernie.

Michael owed Tate a favour after she'd compered his 2006 benefit gig for nurses in character as Bernie. 'He did a concert for NHS nurses and asked me to go on as Bernie because he really liked the show,' she explained. 'I asked if he'd do something for my show and he said "yes".'

Having been a bit of a Wham! fan herself, Tate seemed over the moon for the opportunity to lock lips with her heart-throb, despite his sexuality: 'A model once got to snog George in a very raunchy video for *I Want Your Sex*, and I was always very jealous of her. But after doing these sketches with George, I feel I've evened the score.'

Welsh singer and tabloid legend Charlotte Church also made a guest appearance as the celebrity talent at Nan's Christmas party.

Tate had only good things to say about the woman who is rarely out of the headlines, often for her wild partying ways and refusal to conform to people's expectations: 'She's lovely. She's completely up for a laugh and really down to earth – exactly like you'd imagine. She's a very good actress. I mean she's playing herself – I didn't make her play a Dickensian midwife or anything like that. But she's very natural.'

Nan, of course, had a very different reaction to the star telling her in no uncertain terms: 'Every time I see you in them magazines you're as pissed as an arsehole!'

In terms of comic talent queuing up to appear, it doesn't get much stronger than Peter Kay (who does a duet with Nan as character Tommy Upson), Paul Whitehouse and Kathy Burke. Kay won the hearts of the nation with his *Phoenix Nights* series set in a Northern working men's club and his storming stand-up routines. Whitehouse first became popular as Harry Enfield's sidekick and went on to further fame in *The Fast Show*. And the legend that is Burke appeared as Nan's daughter Diane in a Christmas special, an inspired piece of casting if ever there was one. Said Tate afterwards: 'It was brilliant. When we were thinking who we could have to play the daughter there was really only one person. We didn't think for a minute we'd have a chance, but she wanted to. I was delighted. She's an idol of mine.'

It seems that former *EastEnders* stars couldn't wait to get a look in either with Tamzin Outhwaite (Melanie), Kacey Ainsworth (Little Mo), Patsy Palmer (Bianca), Jill Halfpenny (Kate) and Natalie Cassidy (Sonia) all showing up and proving they were game for a laugh.

And in the kitsch department there was musical theatre star Bonnie Langford, actress Una Stubbs, singers Chas and Dave, and comedy legend Leslie 'Hell-o' Phillips.

However, for sheer 'A' list amazement, there was no-one to beat the current James Bond and hunk-about-town, Daniel Craig. He was persuaded to appear in a *Comic Relief* sketch featuring the unlucky in love but eternally optimistic Elaine Figgis. With her cannibalistic husband dead by lethal injection, and her Egyptian lover long gone with her life savings, she meets 'BondBoy68' on the internet as they bond over a shared love of Celine Dion. Her complete indifference to having this real heart-throb in her living room is what makes this so hilarious. As she confides to the documentary crew: 'He says he's an actor but I've never heard of him,' and later, before she chucks him, 'He's a lovely chap but he's no John Nettles.' Elaine obviously had a preference for the elderly actor who stars in ITV murder mystery series *Midsomer Murders*. In fact, it was when Googling *Midsomer Murders* that she came across her first husband, the convicted murderer on death row.

*

This mastery of comic phrasing, combined with an avowed perfectionism, is what makes Catherine Tate so good at what she does. But she has admitted that her protective attitude to her own creations can make her a difficult colleague: 'I'm probably a pain in the arse to work with, but I care about the show. I'm always ready for a fight. I don't need to be, but I am. It can make for rather a tense atmosphere sometimes. I want everything done five minutes ago. I'll ask, "Why can't we have that crane shot?" without realizing the ceiling is only twelve feet high. I hope I know my limitations, but, generally, I do think I am right all the time.'

She says that, over time, she has gained more confidence in her own abilities: 'I've learned to trust my instincts. If I find something funny, there's a good chance others will too.'

She is glad, too, that success didn't come too soon: 'I wouldn't have been ready for it. I didn't have the confidence. I was thirty-four when the show came out. I knew who I was. I'd had a child. If it had happened earlier I might be jaded now, whereas I think it's really incredible.'

Given the huge success of the three series and the two Christmas specials, it seems a shame that it's unlikely we'll see Nan, Lauren, Derek et al again. She has never publicly confirmed that there will never be another series of *The Catherine Tate Show* but all indications seem to point that way. When *Heat* magazine asked her about the rumours that there were to be no more series at the end of 2006 she said, 'No, I've never said that. I would never be so arrogant to a) assume the BBC would want one, and b) turn it down before they've offered it. There's not another series in the pipeline just because I'm having a break really. It's not like I've closed the door on it. I'm just mindful of not wanting it to outstay its welcome.'

Nearly two years on and there are still no plans for a fourth series, nor has a rumoured touring live show ever materialized. It's possible that she'll do the odd special to keep all her fans happy over Christmas, but at the moment she's pursuing a broader path.

With high profile theatre roles, films and other television projects being offered, you can't blame the woman for wanting to break away from the lovable monsters she's been inhabiting for the best part of three years. At forty, she appears to have decided that scraping her hair back and pretending to be fifteen won't keep her warm, or creatively satisfied, forever more.

CHAPTER SIX

Characters

Lauren Cooper aka Fly Girl

Perhaps the most famous of all Catherine Tate's creations, Lauren is a fifteen-year-old schoolgirl who takes stroppy to a whole new level. Defensive beyond all belief, her sullen attitude can soon turn into a seemingly endless monologue of abuse and justification.

You know things have taken a turn for the worse when she comes out with 'Am I bovvered?' as this question will be repeated with endless, inventive variations until the other person is worn down to a shadow of their former selves. Teachers especially must beware of all they say and all they wear as her attention, once aroused, is like a machine-gun in its lack of mercy.

One woman, who will probably never wear Jesus sandals again, was on the receiving end of: 'Are you a Christian, Miss? Is the Lord your shepherd, Miss? Have you got Jesus in your heart, Miss? Do you like Cliff Richard, Miss? Are you the Vicar of Dibley, Miss? Are we your flock, Miss? Do you have a friend in Jesus, Miss? Does he want you for a sunbeam, Miss?"

Lauren's partners in crime are Ryan and Liese, and the trio will greet all comers with a chorus of 'Aaaal-riiiight!' They're not afraid of taking the Mickey out of her, though, and any blunders on Lauren's part will be met with cries of 'Take the shame!' Mixing up 'bling bling' with 'bing bing' and confusing Dizzee Rascal with Naughty Rascal were just two of her more humiliating moments, which were met, of course, with her stock response of 'Am I bovvered though?'

Lauren is also quick to take offence, assuming that anyone who speaks to her is adopting an attitude of disrespect not only to her but to her entire family. 'Are you disrespectin' me? Are you disrespectin' my family? Are you calling my mum a Pikey? Are you calling my dad a wino?' There really is no way of responding to her quick-fire questions so it really is best just to give up.

With the middle names Alesha, Masheka, Tanesha, Felicia and Jane, it's unsurprising that she has some serious issues. She does make it down the aisle with on-off boyfriend Ryan, though, only to be jilted when she reveals the weakness of her singing voice by trying to belt out her own version of Celine Dion's *My Heart Will Go On*.

Sadly, it didn't go on for that long, as Lauren is believed to have perished in a kayaking accident on a school field trip to Dorset. However, that wasn't before she'd just accused a fisherman of being a 'local yokel', before disappearing over a waterfall.

On her gravestone it reads: 'I Still Ain't Bovvered.'

Nan

One of the most terrifying elderly people you'll ever meet, Nan, also known as Joannie Taylor, can switch from sweetness and light to bitter ranting with one thump on her floral chair. The signs that she's about to switch from sweet old dear to rancid old bag include the trademark thump, a sharp intake of breath that often sounds like 'hup' and the cry of 'What a fucking liberty!'

Her long-suffering foil is grandson, Jamie, who keeps on visiting her despite her foul mouth, sudden temper tantrums and tendency to turn on him at will. Seeming to think that being at university is code for being homosexual, she makes a variety of snide remarks to this effect.

Her bile is not reserved for anyone in particular though. She can turn it on everyone, from the home help to the TV repairman, a doctor's receptionist, a well-meaning nurse, and her own daughter Diane (played by Kathy Burke as a carbon copy of the old woman).

She'll never spit her insults in anyone's face though, instead reserving it all for poor Jamie's ears, and then blaming him for coming up with these crazy ideas in the first place.

Another favourite phrase is 'What a load of old shit!' which was her parting shot when she appeared as a contestant on Noel Edmonds' Channel 4 gameshow, *Deal Or No Deal*.

Derek Faye

About as far in the closet as you can get without being one of its actual fixtures and fittings, Derek Faye is an outrageously camp bald gentleman who insists loudly to anyone who suggests otherwise that he is not a homosexual.

'Gay, dear? Who, dear? Me, dear? No, dear!' is his rallying cry, projected with outrage to anyone who makes this lazy assumption. From his family doctor to his local newsagent, his well-meaning niece to a travel agent organizing a holiday to Ibiza, anyone who even hints that he might be gay gets the sharp end of his tongue.

The facts that he carries a gentleman's sponge bag at all times, still lives with his mother, and is usually seen in the company of his best friend Leonard Mincing, are to no avail. 'How *very* dare you!' he huffs, 'What on *earth* are you insinuating?'

Any suggestions that he's a 'backdoor Deirdre,' 'takes deliveries up the back passage,' or 'travels on the chocolate escalator' will unleash a torrent of terribly inventive abuse. 'Just because a gentleman wears a little foundation, you accuse him of hiding the sausage!' he says, before coming back to pick up his copy of *Hot Muscle* magazine.

Frightened Woman — Margaret, the Screamer

The slightest noise will send this very on-edge housewife into screaming fits. After her husband very quietly sets his tea back in his saucer and takes a discreet bite of toast, she complains that their kitchen is 'like Piccadilly Circus'. God forbid what happens after she pours milk on her bowl of Rice Krispies.

The phone ringing, a gentle sneeze or a musical card will have her shattering the air with piercing cries that can be heard beyond a two-hundred-mile radius. It's not just noise that sets her off though. Watch out for the ear-shattering cacophony that greets her husband when he turns on the Christmas tree lights.

Botox Babe

A blonde American actress shooting a legal thriller called *Guilty Promise*, Botox Babe makes an alarming transformation over night. One day, we are witness to an intimate scene being shot with co-star Michael Brandon (Dempsey from *Dempsey and Makepeace*). As the action picks up the next day, a shiny pink trout-pout of enormous proportions emerges from her blonde hair. Brandon is the only one completely thrown by this terrifying cosmetic enhancement, and looks like a man heading for the gas chamber as he's forced to go in for the screen kiss.

Aga Saga Woman

Living in the height of luxury and comfort somewhere safe and Sloaney in central London, Aga Saga Woman finds that the most trifling of problems sends her into a terminal tizz. The trouble is, along the way she also panics her two perfectly blonde children, Thomas and Chloe.

Just some of the problems that beset this perfect family are Papa not being able to fetch back a decent Brie from his business trip to Paris, being forced to use a hire car, the use of non-organic eggs at the school egg and spoon race, and a gooseberry and cinnamon yoghurt past its sell-by date. All of these crises spark the reaction: 'Oh my God! We're all going to die!'

Best of all, though, is the shock replacement nanny from the agency who is from 'the North'! Not being able to understand one word of her Geordie accent, Aga Saga Woman and her family all run away screaming under the mistaken impression that she's out to murder them in their beautiful London home.

New Parents

As they've got a six-month-old baby who is a stranger to sleep, the New Parents turn into the bickering, anti-social couple from hell. They force their friends to eat dinner in their car for fear of waking the baby, and they rip up a singing birthday card in a fit of temper because it belts out *Congratulations* when they open it.

They only break off from a feverish exchange of insults – one example being, 'Concentrate on the road, you evil little dwarf!' – to sing a sweet duet of *Loving You Was Easier* to soothe their fractious infant.

Drunken Bride

Clearly not terribly happy to have finally made it up the aisle with her besotted groom, John, Victoria Russell has fifteen too many at the reception and insists on making an embarrassing speech.

Highlights of this include admitting to having slept with thirty-nine men, suggesting that John isn't terribly well-endowed, calling his mother fat, and bringing up his sister's problems with bulimia. All of this ends up with her being passed out in a darkened reception venue. Alone.

Snack Food Woman

Addicted to little bags of savoury snacks, this woman excuses herself from situations at the last minute to pop down to the newsagents and get her fix. When she returns with her bag of Mini Cheddars or Nik Naks, she always finds that some terrible disaster has befallen her companions in the meantime. These include a block of flats falling on her boyfriend's head, and her best friend perishing in a drive-by shooting. Maybe those hydrogenated fats have their uses after all.

Frankie Howerd Impressionist

A serious actress shooting serious scenes with her co-stars, this woman has a tendency to break into an impersonation of camp comic Frankie Howerd at the most inopportune moments. Seemingly unaware that she is doing it, she confuses her fellow actors and directors by launching into 'Ooh-er missus' during love scenes and labour scenes alike.

Crap Croupier

Hardly the ultimate professional, this is a croupier who can't stand the noise of the ball spinning on the roulette wheel. She also has a tendency to whip the ball off the wheel before it lands as she gets bored, and announcing to gamblers that it's landed on one colour when, in fact, it's landed on the opposite. Finally, watching the wheel spinning too closely causes her to faint dead away.

How Much / How Many

We've all had colleagues who refuse to let us get on with our work in peace but the How Much/ How Many woman takes the cake – and then shoves it in your face. Sporting a blonde bob and an annoying pout, she tortures the woman sitting next to her with endless requests for her to guess some aspect of her day-to-day life.

Whether it's how much weight she's lost, how many extras were used in *Ben Hur*, how long it took her to get to Cornwall or where her hairdresser is from, she won't impart the information without first getting the beleaguered woman to hazard a guess. And her guesses are all usually so way out that it inspires her total outrage. When her workmate guesses that she's run thirty miles in a morning she responds: 'Thirty miles in one go? Do I look Ethiopian?'

When occasionally her colleague gets it right, this usually inspires some petty revenge like shoving all her files off her desk.

Not Drunk Enough

Surely a man's idea of the worst date ever is this self-possessed woman who simply can't drink enough to make herself want to sleep with him. Having already taken her to the Munich beer festival (where she drank her own body weight in lager), he's running out of ideas.

In the worst backhanded compliment ever uttered, she says she would fancy him 'if only I could get so spectacularly pissed that I wasn't aware of what you looked like.'

Not one to have his ego bruised easily or to give up without a fight, he hands her a can of Special Brew and suggests that she gives him a call. If only her liver weren't so damaged already that doctors have given her under a year to live.

Paul and Sam

An Essex couple who crack themselves up with the most banal of anecdotes, this is a pair who are truly in love and truly deserve each other.

'You're mental, you are!' Paul says fondly as Sam recounts yet another dizzy escapade involving choosing the wrong sandwich, ringing the wrong friend, or getting the wrong end of the stick. There is nothing that won't reduce this couple to helpless fits of giggles and self-congratulatory statements.

We eventually get to meet their children in a Christmas special and, luckily for all concerned, they have exactly the same personalities as their 'kerazy' parents.

Enigmatic Cop

Well and truly taking the Michael out of all those television dramas featuring maverick female detectives, Enigmatic Cop is a woman Detective Inspector who makes no sense at all.

She puzzles viewers and her trusty anorak-wearing sidekick, Whittaker, with a series of ridiculous statements relating to the murders they're investigating. When confronted with a lifeless corpse, she begins musing as to whether he's actually dead before launching into a passionate rendition of The Pretenders' *Brass In*

Pocket, expecting Whittaker to join in at key moments.

As she later asks him to shoot her through the heart with the murder weapon, it's no surprise that his favourite response is, 'I'm not exactly sure where you're going with this, ma'am.'

Information Woman

If you're ever lost or looking for assistance in a shopping mall, this is the last woman you'd want to encounter. Supremely unhelpful not by dint of attitude but rather by her spectacular ability to miss the point, she sends away customers more confused than when they arrived.

When a woman fetches up at the counter to explain that she's lost her mum, Information Woman unhelpfully enquires 'Did she have a good innings?' and then goes back to perusing her glossy magazine. Further bids for help are finally met with 'You can usually smell them can't you?' She's not talking about muffins but old people.

A woman attempting to return a jumper to a shop that's closed down is met with 'Thanks, but I don't think it would suit me,' while a man looking for a window replacement service is referred to a firm some hundreds of miles away in Leeds. 'I need a professional,' he says.

'You mean like a hit man?' is her reply.

Bernie

A red-headed Irish nurse with a sex drive greater than Hugh Hefner's, Bernie is the bane of Sister's life. She'll happily proposition any man with a pulse, from patients to doctors to random visitors and is always on the look-out for a dirty great ride. You definitely wouldn't want her looking after you if you were languishing in bed with a serious medical problem, but you'd sure as hell want her with you on a night out on the lash.

Her crimes range from photo-copying her bottom to taking an eighty-one-year-old patient to see *Chitty Chitty Bang Bang*, giving a man with liver disease a cocktail called 'Screaming Orgasm' and lying in patients' beds and eating their chocolates.

With the motto 'I don't kiss and tell. I shag and shout!', it's no wonder that she was advised to address a feminine problem with live yoghurt. With only a Mueller Crunch Corner to hand, however she confides: 'The chafing I've had all morning.'

Having managed to resist the lesbian advances of a fellow nurse at the last Christmas party, she manages to cop off with George Michael at the next one, after singing with him a duet of the Pogues' classic *Fairytale of New York* at the karaoke night.

Watch out for her sisters Bridie and Brenda as they appear to be even scarier.

Drunk Estate Agent

While it's rare to find a popular estate agent, you'll hopefully never run into one as nightmarish as this squiffy creation.

Showing a couple of prospective buyers around a terribly nice house with the lovely lady owner, she manages to insult all three in spectacular fashion. Not being able to remember what she valued the property for, she then knocks ten grand off, based on her opinion that the buyers will need to spend at least a couple of grand to 'get rid of the smell of sex'.

Having compared the brand new pull-out kitchen units with the morgue in *Silent Witness*, she then goes on to tell the husband that he's 'a big old bender'. This is based solely on his cropped hairstyle, cheap aftershave and love of chrome in the kitchen.

Her final line is the best. Told that 'you are a disgrace to your profession,' she slurs back, 'Don't be ridiculous. I'm an estate agent.'

Elaine Figgis — Death Row Wife

A resident of Leeds, thirty-four-year-old Elaine Figgis works part-time in a bakery and spends her spare hours corresponding with her fiancé, Jeremiah Wainwright the Third.

Also known as 'The Cleaver', Jeremiah is languishing on Death Row in Texas, awaiting death by lethal injection as punishment for abducting, murdering and torturing eight people. He also ate two of them, something that the very tolerant Elaine is prepared to overlook. 'He ate a bit of one of them,' she says. 'When he was a student, which is a time when most of us are experimenting with something new.'

Elaine heads off on a four-thousand-mile journey to wed her man in a Texas jail. There is no kissing, however, due to the fact that he has to be heavily sedated and is required to wear a muzzle twenty-four-hours a day.

Unfortunately, she is his wife for only five days before he gets sent for execution. Elaine marks this with a moving ceremony in her Leeds council house, marred only by the fact that the candle she has bought to blow out at his moment of passing is one of those joke self-lighting ones used on birthday cakes.

Elaine lives on to love another day, falling for an Egyptian named Mohammed who takes her for every penny. She almost gets a happy ending though, when James Bond actor Daniel Craig falls for her statuesque charms.

As she puts it though: 'He's no John Nettles'.

Bunty

The oldest majorette in the land, Bunty Carmichael refuses to retire from the Doncaster Spinners despite the best efforts of manager Geoff.

In a series of increasingly painful meetings over several pints of real ale in the local pub, Geoff tries to persuade Bunty that it really is time for her to hang up her baton. At thirty-one, she just doesn't fit in any more. 'Without you, the average age of the team would be twelve,' he says.

Yet for Bunty, dubbed the 'Twirlminator' at a long-ago contest, twirling is everything: 'I love spinning a baton. It's me life," she says. Refusing to get the message, Bunty takes to stalking the team wearing a false nose and moustache and eventually has to be served with a restraining order after chaining herself to school railings and singing Bon Jovi's *Living On A Prayer* in a one-woman protest.

She ends each tragic meeting with Geoff by selecting a heart-felt tune on the jukebox – tugging our and Geoff's heartstrings with everything from Eric Carmen's *All By Myself* to Culture Club's *Do You Really Want To Hurt Me?*

Valley Girl

Rather like an American version of Lauren, this blonde and extremely inarticulate young American lady talks us through her encounters with the opposite sex as she sits in a classic diner.

Her remarks all run along the lines of 'So, I'm, like, ooh and he's, like, what, and I'm, like, dude and he's, like, babe and I'm, like, OK, and he's, like, supremo, and I'm, like, uh-oh.'

All these encounters start out well and end rather badly in a flurry of incomprehension.

Backhander Woman

Looking as if butter wouldn't melt in her mouth, and with a cute little fringe held back by a sparkly butterfly clip, this woman packs a mighty punch.

When faced with a vegetarian café worker, a roadside windscreen washer, or a mime artist in the park, she startles her companions with the strength of her responses. Launching into a vitriolic attack on each, essayed in lovingly violent detail, she ends each tirade with the suggestion that a backhander in the gob would do them the world of good.

'Hitler-worshipping Pikey scum!' and 'What in the name of Christ are you doing with your life?' are just some of her milder utterances.

Last Hit Woman

A businesswoman in a high-powered firm, manager Sandra Graham just can't resist touching everyone she knows, shouting 'last hit' and running away.

When her employee Tony decides to beat her at her own game, things take a tragic turn. He's run over trying to get the better of her, and she ends up chasing the ambulance as he rouses himself to give her one 'last hit'.

After she bonks him on the head in his hospital bed, he ends up dying but not before he tells his wife to pass on one last message to Sandra...

This causes Sandra to try and throw herself into his open grave in an attempt to get the absolute 'last hit'.

Lady Clown

Gill is the greatest challenge the leader of the Clown Skills Workshop has ever faced, and is fighting to forget the fact that she once killed a man in a car accident.

When she practises the clown tripping-up routine, it reminds her of how she was found slumped over her steering wheel; and she really wishes the victim could have been wearing her purple curly wig as then she might have seen him in time. She makes her face-painting child up as an accident victim, and when it comes to balloon-twisting, she comes up with a noose rather than a giraffe.

Martin Webb

Martin is the epitome of every annoying git who's ever bored you to death with his mobile phone conversations on public transport.

On his way back from an awards do in London, Martin rings up all of his unenthusiastic work colleagues one by one to fill them in on the gory details. Strangely, neither his fellow passengers nor his workmates back at the office want to hear how he got hammered on 'cham-pag-nay', bought a two-hundred-quid suit on Oxford Street, and slept with a prostitute.

Ali Inappropriate Woman

Personifying the inner social fool in all of us, Ali comes straight out and says exactly the wrong thing at the wrong time. Why her friends continue to invite her to the parties that she's constantly attending will remain one of life's great mysteries.

With a jolly-dee approach, she comes across as perfectly harmless and fun. Harmless and fun, that is, until she opens her mouth and inserts her foot straight into it without passing 'Go' or collecting that leaving certificate from charm school.

Ali tries to remove a hair from a woman's face that's actually growing out of it, tells a man to rub an embarrassing stain from his head that's really a birthmark, asks a man with a Kevin Keegan-esque curly perm if she can take his hat, and assumes that a deaf man who is signing is actually trying to engage her in a game of charades.

If you have a tendency to open your mouth without first engaging your brain, Ali would be the perfect decoy to take along on social occasions when you wished to remain under the radar. With her and her big mouth around, no-one will be looking at you.

I Can Do That Woman

We've all come across those annoying people who claim they can do anything from navigate their way to the North Pole without a compass to whip up a five-course, Michelin-star meal.

Here is that woman who gets herself into all sorts of embarrassing scrapes by claiming to have skills far greater than she actually possesses. Not that it stops her trying again – shame and this woman are strangers.

So, she fails to hit a ball on the tennis court despite claiming to be tournament standard, she makes a total arse of herself on a curling team by falling on her own too often, speaks gibberish to foreign visitors instead of translating the seven languages she claims to speak, and shakes like an incontinent jelly at salsa dance classes.

Life At Ma's – Ma Willow and Sam Speed

A hommage to *Life On Mars*, the popular time-travelling police drama that took us back to Manchester in the 1970s, this miniseries sees modern-day cop Sam Speed catapulted back to the 1950s.

Here he is forced to take lodging with Ma Willow, a Cockney landlady who is fond of serving up tripe and onions, chain-smoking and having a good-old sing song round the old Joanna with her friends. Sam is horrified at their diet and lifestyle, telling them they won't live past sixty if they carry on like this, remarks which receive gales of laughter and a cheery 'I hope not dear.'

Philip Glenister, who played Gene Hunt in the original series, pops up as a 1950s seaside cop forced to arrest Sam for the brevity of his bathing trunks.

24 And A Half – Laura Powers, Rubbish Spy

A spoof of the smash-hit American series 24, this introduces us to British spy, Laura Powers, on board at the CTQ HQ in Houston, Texas.

Her American boss tells her, 'It's good to have the British with us,' a statement he comes to regret when Laura proves to have a useless grasp of technology and no clue whatsoever how to do anything. As the clock ticks away, and a hijacked plane threatens to explode, she proves utterly hopeless at doing anything about it, unable even to find the 'J' on her keyboard.

John Leary's Mum

Kathleen Leary is a hard-faced Northern Irish woman who doesn't suffer fools gladly. But when her nervous son John manages to spit out the fact that he's gay over the tea table, she couldn't be more delighted and takes him straight upstairs to advise her what her hips look like in a pencil skirt.

Her avid support of his newly-revealed sexuality brings nothing but embarrassment to John as she tells all and sundry and the local priest: 'Have you heard the news? Our John's a gay man now.'

She makes his face turn puce as he watches football with his mates by leafing through magazines to find hunky male torsos and opining, 'Look at the buns on that John.' It seems that even the local hard men are unfazed by John's sexuality as they turn up on his door seeking fashion advice about how their turn-ups look with their bovver boots.

John Leary's mum's finest hour, though, is undoubtedly when she joins him on a Gay Pride march.

The Annoying Waitress — Amanda Zebedee

An unnaturally cheerful server at one of those Technicolored chain burger joints, this woman tests the patience of even the saintliest customers.

With a jaunty 'My name's Amanda but my friends call me Zebedee. I'm a fiery Taurean with my moon in Uranus. Careful! I'll do the jokes,' she sets the tone for a hideous dining experience. Anyone who orders fries gets treated to a chorus of 'One potato, two potato, three potato, four,' while a request for the 'Oops Upside Your Head' burger brings all the servers to their table for an action replay of the 1970s classic.

Anyone with an ounce of fat will also be informed: 'I've been asked to point out to our more generously proportioned customers that when we say the Hawaiian buffet is all you can eat, that is in fact an offer, not a challenge."

Beware of the Boogie Dogs too as they will prompt a rousing rendition of the Nolan Sisters' *I'm In The Mood For Dancing*.

Moo Shepherd — Dog Trainer

After the death of her beloved dog, Mr Tibbs – 'He was to training and obedience what Patrick Swayze was to the power ballad' – Moo Shepherd is forced to train another pooch. Unfortunately her new dog, Lady Penelope, doesn't even understand 'sit', so Moo's chances of being eight times winner of the Midlands Six Part Obedience Championship are looking anorexic.

A hard task mistress – she once made a woman eat a tin of dog food for being ten minutes late to one of her obedience classes – she battles on, nearly finishing Lady Penelope off with an electronic pulse gadget in the pursuit of her dream. Her love of quoting pop lyrics from the likes of Michael Jackson, Will Young and Wham! may well save her from herself.

Sheila Carter — Scottish Farter

A prissy Scottish woman of a certain vintage, Sheila Carter turns a disapproving eye on the behaviour of all those around her.

She lectures the occupants of a funeral car on their inappropriate language, whistling and mobile phone usage before letting out the most enormous and unapologetic fart. This she doesn't acknowledge, rather telling the man next to her to move down as 'it's very stuffy in here.' This anti-social behaviour is repeated in a poor man's taxi cab after he's been told off about his air freshener and his choice of radio stations, and in a confessional box at the local church.

Ginger Woman — Sandra Kemp

We first see Sandra in a police station being comforted about the appalling injustices and discrimination she has faced. It's only after a few minutes that we realize that it is her red hair that is the cause of the campaign of harassment against her.

A victim in a society that is horribly gingerist, Sandra is taken into protective custody for her own good. Her destination? Russet Lodge, a safe house where everyone from strawberry blondes to flame-haired sirens can live in peace and harmony. Allegedly.

While Sandra might object to being 'put in the ghetto', here everyone is trained to work with ginger people and some even have ginger relatives. Later, Sandra will rise up and form the 'Gingers For Justice' campaign, staging a roof top protest that attracts red-headed *EastEnders* actress Patsy Palmer to join in dressed as a Duracell battery. But can they persuade the public not to be so gingerphobic?

Irene and Vernon — Burger Van

This unlikely couple run a burger van in an anonymous lay-by. Vernon copes by never uttering a word while wife Irene makes her days bearable by pretending that all sorts of unlikely celebrities have popped by for a double cheeseburger with extra onions.

She regales their only customer Neville (Brian Murphy of *George and Mildred* fame) with tales of her latest high-profile customers. Madonna pops in on her way to the garden centre and bangs on about Iraq, Desmond Tutu wants to know where the nearest Halfords is so he can replace the Calor gas can in the caravan he's borrowed from the Archbishop of Canterbury, while American politician Condoleezza Rice is visiting relatives in the area.

Angie Barker – The new DI with three kids in tow

Another pop at those television crime dramas featuring maverick women detectives, Angie Barker is a working mum and solver of murders who brings her three kids along to the scenes of the crime. Much to the horror of her colleagues, the kids bounce up and down on the corpse of a murdered prostitute and generally have a whale of a time contaminating evidence.

Ivan and Trudy – Dodd's Wigmakers

They may have covered the most famous of scalps with their hair pieces, but Ivan and Trudy, wigmakers to the stars, have their professional reputation to consider.

The subject of a fly-on-the-wall documentary, they desperately try and hide their client list from the snooping television crew. All their best efforts are foiled by blabbermouth receptionist

Carol-Ann (Una Stubbs), however, as she keeps forgetting the camera is switched on and blurting out customers' names. Among her 'bald' revelations are Delia Smith, Helen Mirren and Dame Judi Dench.

Blowsy Trudy and camp-as-Christmas Ivan have a frosty relationship, mostly owing to the fact that he seems far more interested in muscle-bound Latin American assistant Bruno than he does in her.

Geordie Georgie

The most irritating North-Easterner ever to have walked among us, Geordie Georgie is another contender in line for the Colleague From Hell award.

Georgie greets her co-worker every day with a cheery 'Mornin' Martin.' This is usually preceded by a song as she enters the office and then asks to borrow some item of his stationery. She then launches into her latest and increasingly bizarre charity appeal, attempting to persuade the hapless Martin to part with yet more of his hard-earned cash.

Whatever she is fund-raising for – and her range encompasses battered husbands from Gateshead (www.chinnedbythemissus. co.uk), sexually harassed workers (www.bummedbytheboss. co.uk), victims of obsessive-compulsive disorder (www.christive-lefttheovenon.co.uk/noihavent/yesihave) and alcoholics in Jarrow (www.ifuckingloveyou.co.uk/haveitoldyouifuckingloveyou) – her pitch is a hard one. If Martin attempts to resist, or only give her a small amount of cash, her retribution is both swift and violent.

She gets her comeuppance during a *Comic Relief* sketch, though. when Lenny Henry pops by to collect for a far better and more plausible cause than she's ever been able to come up with.

Janice and Ray

A parochial Yorkshire couple approaching late middle age, Janice and Ray are outraged at every turn by food that doesn't conform to their very strict views of what 'proper' food should be.

Sitting on a floral sofa and addressing an unseen interviewer, they reel off in great detail the latest outrage that has greeted their delicate palates. Food stuffs that have excited their ire include dried shitake mushrooms – 'I mean dried, shit ache, mushrooms' – a cheese sandwich that involved Brie, French bread and, horror of horrors, grapes, and goat curry with plantain at a shopping centre in Cleethorpes.

Special disgust is reserved for a pub in Leeds that no longer serves chips and instead specializes in Thai food. When their suggested order of vegetable tempura turns out to be 'Battered veg! With spicy jam!' there's no telling what Ray will do.

Each description is rounded off with the horrified exclamation: 'The dirty bastards!'

CHAPTER SEVEN

The Trials of Motherhood

One of the saddest parts of Catherine Tate's long awaited but very sudden success was her inability to relish every minute of it. When the BBC told her that they were going ahead and commissioning the very first series of *The Catherine Tate Show*, she was pregnant with her daughter Erin and had just finished filming *Wild West* with Dawn French.

Life should have been glorious for the then thirty-five-year-old who had spent years working towards her goals of career fulfilment and recognition. But she has admitted that depression began to overtake her from the day she found out she was pregnant and that, hiding it from friends and family, she filmed the entire first series while suffering from postnatal depression.

Watching the first series and seeing the joy and comedy in those characters, it's almost impossible to imagine that the woman who created them and brought them to life was going through a living hell. If anyone doubted her serious acting abilities, and dismissed her as a mere comedienne, then this knowledge alone should have dispelled those preconceptions.

But let's go back to when she first met her partner, stage manager Twig Clark, in 2000. They were both working at the Royal Shakespeare Company at the time and she has joked: 'I was on tour and he was one of the crew. I thought he was a YTS [Youth Training Scheme] boy. Then I saw he was a hunk, trapped him, and got pregnant!'

They met on an RSC tour that took them around the world for a year and, by the time they got back, they'd fallen in love. The tour included the play *A Servant To Two Masters* and took in the US, Hong Kong and Israel as well as Australia. These must have been exciting times given the exotic locations, the close-knit nature of working with a travelling group of actors and the distinct possibility of romance. She claimed in a *Guardian* questionnaire that working in Australia in 2001 was when, and where, she was happiest, and later admitted, shyly: 'It was a lovely time. I had a great job and we visited Australia, Hong Kong and America and when we got back Twig still liked me.'

They have been a couple ever since and she became pregnant in 2002, although it was unplanned. Giving press interviews after she filmed *Wild West* while still pregnant, there was no sign of her depression or anxiety, and she seemed as blown away to be working with the illustrious Dawn French as she was about impending motherhood.

Watching the first series of *Wild West* with foreknowledge, it is obvious that she's pregnant. 'I think we managed to get away with my pregnancy during filming. I wore big coats and there was always a chair and a glass of water not too far away. I only found out I was pregnant after I had got the part. We had to use a stunt double during the fight scenes but apart from that everything was fine.'

She did admit to the enormity of the upheaval to her life, however, what with a starring role in a BBC sitcom and a baby on the way. 'I don't have one major life-changing event to deal with – I have two,' she said at the time. 'But landing my biggest job and having a baby at the same time has meant that my life has not been dominated by either one. The pregnancy wasn't planned. I always saw myself becoming a mother, just not at this point. It looks like I got on the fast track to motherhood.'

While she made these comments very light-heartedly at the time, it became clear later that this fast track to both fame and motherhood was far too much to cope with. She also speculated on how she would feel about returning to work after the birth, hoping that she wouldn't feel the need to do so right away. 'I want to go back to work after having the baby, but I think it is sad that some women feel a pressure to rush back to work for fear of getting forgotten. I have friends who have decided to take a lot of time off after having a baby and found themselves tearing their hair out at home, and others who have gone back to work too quickly and find they are torn between their job and missing their baby.'

She was also quick to point out that she dreaded turning into a caricature of a stay-at-home mum and didn't anticipate becoming an earth mother either: 'I can't see myself as the sort of woman who gets into cardigans and wanting to puree carrots. I want to get back to work but without sacrificing the well-being of the baby.'

Lest there be any misunderstanding, there was certainly no question of the baby being unwanted. She and Twig had even discussed the possibility of him changing his highly unusual first name for fear of their child suffering any stigma by association. He apparently came by his name by way of very unorthodox parents. 'At one time Twig's parents were hippies,' she's explained, 'and I think his dad believed he was a tree so Twig must have seemed like an obvious choice.'

It seems that bearing such a remarked-upon name has not been without its problems, however: 'His name has caused him a lot of heartache over the years. When he starts a new job he knows that by the second day people will start asking him what his real name is. When we discovered that I was pregnant Twig even considered changing his name by deed poll because we didn't want our son or daughter suffering when they started school because of their dad's name.'

When her daughter was born in February 2003, there was no question of calling her 'Bud' or 'Leaf' though she did very nearly end up being called Eugene. 'I was so shocked that she was a girl,' Tate said afterwards, 'I had completely expected I was going to have a little, pale, ginger boy who I would have to call Eugene or something. I couldn't believe it – she had this thatch of dark hair, though she is now blonde.'

Given their surprise at the sex of the baby, and having not trawled through lists of books for girls' names, the couple then struggled to come up with an appropriate moniker. 'We nearly got sent one of those summonses because we had not registered a name. We'd call her a different name every day to see if it stuck.

But no matter which name we tried, nothing stuck, it was so weird. Then I looked through a book of names and saw Erin and it just seemed really nice. It's Irish and there is an Irish connection in the family, way back to great-great grandmothers. I am Irish and Scottish. But that wasn't the reason for her name.'

*

However lightly Tate talks about this period after the birth of her daughter, we know now how dark those days were as she has discussed openly her living nightmare. As mentioned before, the depression wasn't just postnatal, but began from the day she discovered she was going to become a mother. 'It started the moment I got pregnant,' she told the *Daily Telegraph*, 'I felt totally and completely trapped, which was just so unexpected because my game plan had always included children. People would ring up and go, aren't you just walking on air? And I'd think, well, no actually, I'm not, although I never said it. It got worse when she was born. I had an emergency Caesarean and I couldn't breast feed and we didn't bond at all, so for the first six months of her life she was raised by my mum and my boyfriend because I just... couldn't.'

This is obviously a source of huge remorse for her and she has said that one of her biggest regrets is that, when she looks back on this period of her daughter's early life, shedoesn't recall much about it.

She is also clearly unhappy at what happened to her in the hospital after her emergency Caesarean when she was totally exhausted and was unable to breast feed properly. 'It was a "baby- friendly hospital", so they refused you formula except in emergencies. So that's how I met a woman who'd given birth the day before, sneaking across the road with her coat over her nightie to buy a carton of SMA at the chemists.'

Her only glimmer of hope came from the visit of a sympathetic nurse in the middle of the night when she was at her lowest ebb. It must have felt like a heavenly visitation to a desperate Tate who could see no hope at this point. Obviously recognizing her condition, as she had seen it many times before, the nurse said: 'You know what? In ten years' time when she's at school, it won't matter.' Tate asked her if she was sure, and then relaxed a little. She has since said: 'Oh my God, I'm very grateful to that woman.'

Things didn't get any better when she got home though, and she was faced with the prospect of having to come up with her first television comedy series. To someone who is feeling fit and competent, this amount of pressure would be just about unbearable, but to a weakened Tate who was in the grips of undiagnosed postnatal depression (PND), it must have been intolerable. 'I was so raw for the first year, it was irrational. I was putting together the first series six months after giving birth, and I couldn't think about it either. I just went on autopilot and waded through my life.'

As she has already said, her partner and her mother Josephine largely assumed responsibility for Erin for the first six months of her life. Twig gave up work to take care of the new baby, although at that time she still hadn't admitted to family or friends the extent of her problem. 'What drove me bananas was trying to hide that from people, because it was too much to put on my family. So the solution was: OK, I'll go and write a comedy show. I hadn't got help for the depression during the first series – I just put it on hold. It wasn't until really the end of series two that I sorted it out. Plus, the second series was worse because I knew the work involved, and I had to raise the bar.'

While postnatal depression is a recognized medical condition, if someone is in the grips of it without realizing what is going on, or without seeking help, then it can be terrifying and very lonely. Women who are high achievers or place a lot of pressure on themselves are also at a higher risk, which would certainly seem to fit in Tate's case.

According to a report in *The Observer*, between ten and twenty per cent of all new mothers are likely to suffer depression, and for a third to a half of these, it will be severe. Two per cent of women will see a psychiatrist during the first year, four in every thousand will be admitted to hospital, and two in every thousand will suffer the most extreme PND, also known as puerperal psychosis.

Often dismissed as the 'baby blues', PND is much more than feeling a little low after giving birth. Doctor Margaret Oates, Chair of the Royal College of Psychiatrists' Perinatal Special Interest Group and head of the pioneering mother and baby unit at Nottingham's Queen's Medical Centre, explains the difference: 'It's a slowing up, impaired concentration; it's profound feelings of guilt and unworthiness that you can't shake off. Your life has all the ingredients to be happy, but you feel an all-pervading sadness. You have horrible, morbid thoughts, perhaps about harming yourself or your baby. Any mother may experience some or all of this at times, but with postnatal depression it doesn't vary. It generally begins at about four to six weeks and gently gathers speed.'

Oates also explains, in layman's terms, the medical reasons for such terrible grief: 'Through pregnancy, the placenta pumps out industrial quantities of hormones, and when it is removed those levels plummet. What happens is a withdrawal effect, just as you get when you stop taking heroin or alcohol or anti depressants.'

It's interesting what Oates has to say about people's lives having 'all the ingredients to be happy' as this is surely another reason why someone as apparently successful as Tate wouldn't want to admit to her negative feelings. Those of us who are less successful may well have reacted with the attitude Tate found so confusing as a child that it's 'alright for some'. How dare a well-known celebrity with a loving partner, a brand new baby and a financial cushion complain of being unhappy?

It's just as well, then, that so many celebrities have now come out and admitted to suffering from PND. As well as raising public awareness and helping less well-known new mums recognize the condition, they've surely paved the way for other celebrities to admit to their illness without fear of censure.

The types of celebrities who have come out about their post-natal depression are wide-ranging. They include everyone from Hollywood notables such as Brooke Shields and Courtney Cox Arquette to music stars like Atomic Kitten's Natasha Hamilton, British gossip magazine favourites Gail Porter, Suzanne Shaw and

Melinda Messenger, supermodel Elle McPherson, actress Sadie Frost, and presenters Fern Britton and Zoë Ball.

From a wide range of ages and backgrounds, these people demonstrate that postnatal depression can affect anyone and their very public statements about it should go a long way toward removing the stigma. Courtney Cox Arquette, who shot to international fame as Monica in American sitcom *Friends*, and had baby Coco with actor husband David Arquette, admitted: 'I went through a really hard time – not right after the baby, but when Coco turned six months. I couldn't sleep. My heart was racing. And I got really depressed. I went to the doctor and found out my hormones had been pummelled.'

Brooke Shields, star of 1980s movies *Endless Love* and *The Blue Lagoon* was moved to write a book called *Down Came The Rain: My Journey Through Postpartum Depression* after giving birth to daughter Rowan, and had a high-profile spat with Scientologist and actor Tom Cruise about whether or not she should have been taking antidepressants.

The wonderfully maternal Fern Britton, star of *This Morning* and mother of four children, went even further when she admitted to suicidal feelings: 'I've had times when I've wished I wouldn't wake up. Yes, I felt suicidal. It's a chemical imbalance. I have taken antidepressants, but I've been really well for ages.'

Sadie Frost, who got postnatal depression in 2002 after her son by Jude Law, Rudy, was born prematurely, sounds like she had exactly the same reaction as Tate: 'I just couldn't cope and found it really hard to talk to anyone. The postnatal depression ate up everything. Looking back, I can't believe I felt like that.'

Tate told *The Daily Telegraph* that it was in the summer of 2004 that she really hit rock bottom. She decided to ignore her doctor's advice that she be hospitalized in a mother and baby unit, and was instead 'sitting at home with the curtains drawn, a tub of ice cream and two boxed sets of *ER*.' She eventually took antidepressants and, by the end of 2004, felt that she had turned a corner.

Yet it seems that she feels her protracted battle with depression has left a lasting mark, taking away her ability to be purely happy again. 'I went to a different place after I had the baby. I don't think I'm ever going to scale the dizzy heights of enthusiasm, the way I might have done in my teens. I don't think you can when you've plumbed such depths – you just manage to keep on a neutral keel. But I do have to remember that all my success, really, has happened in parallel with me being pregnant and having a baby.'

She has compared the fact of her television career taking off at the same time to having twins. 'Things just started getting very busy as I got pregnant and I just managed with it. It is like people who have twins first time – they don't know any different. I have just factored it all in. But there are compromises and maybe for my next baby I will take time off.'

So, she hasn't ruled out another pregnancy, far from it, telling any number of journalists that she'd like to have another child. She has also talked about taking six months off but finds it difficult to turn work down, unable to forget how difficult it was before people started knocking down her door.

She must be fearful, though, of repeating her experience with post natal depression, and has said as much, but also added: 'I hope it won't stop me, because they're brilliant, but it does worry me. Also, I want one because I wouldn't like her to be an only child – I was an only child and I think it's great, but...'

Tate also says that she regrets talking about her illness so openly as she fears it has promoted an image of her as 'the tear-stained clown', a tag she desperately wants to avoid. 'That's so much the image of the crying clown. And I'm not one. I think of what I do as a really great job, but it doesn't bleed into other areas of my life. If I could help other people with it, I would, but I'm not sure the way to do it is to be saying, I had postnatal depression but now I've got a comedy show!'

In fact, she thinks that the depression may have also been a reaction to her simultaneous career success. 'In a funny sort of way I think my depression is a defence mechanism, a reaction to all the good things that have happened, a means, in a way, of reining me in, distancing me from the enormity of it all.'

*

Simply admitting the difficulties of motherhood in the press, rather than promoting a rosy image of it, must have done the world of good to a lot of her fans struggling to cope. Gone are the days when we wanted our favourite celebrities to be picture perfect and beyond reproach in every area of their lives. If we can see that they, too, struggle to cope with the demands of everyday life, then so much the better. It makes us feel less guilty about being far from perfect ourselves.

How many mothers, delirious from lack of sleep, must have

smiled to themselves to read this admission from Tate? 'Erin still doesn't sleep and she is three now. Well, it's not that she doesn't sleep, it's that she sleeps in our bed. And, of course, she will sleep horizontally across it. It means I don't sleep because I am constantly worried she is going to fall out. So what happens is, I go into her bed and sleep on a two-foot Barbie bed, which is why I am so tired.'

Desperate to have their bed back, she and Twig sought help but the solution didn't last: 'We went to a sleep clinic when she was about twenty months old and they were brilliant. They did this thing where, as soon as the baby gets up, you just put her back down and stay with her until she goes to sleep and it worked. But then we moved house and there were new surround-ings...'

Despite her post natal despair, Tate still managed to use some of these experiences to good effect in her sketch show. New mums and dads who saw one of her characters trying not to doze off as she talked her wide-awake baby through alphabet blocks would surely have shared a wry smile. '"K" is for knackered' and '"N" is for no sleep for Mummy.'

Tate has also said that the over-anxious New Parents who go round to their friends' house and insist on eating the whole meal in the car for fear of waking the baby are based on herself and Twig. 'We were martyrs. I think, to your first children you are martyrs. We would live around her nap times in a most pathetic way. God, please God, don't let us be under a flight path today.'

And even though she's recovered from the depression, she still counts herself as an anxious mum and finds herself having the strangest thoughts at the most inappropriate times. She has said that she's thought things like, 'Oh my God, what if she chokes on her Rice Krispies!' and has even had to stop working to phone home and check. Even when she's at home and has her eye on Erin, the worrying doesn't stop: 'Like, she's got these dressing-up shoes, and they're too high for her, and she's going to get blisters, and don't let her go upstairs in them because she'll break her neck...'

*

One major television project she has done since she brought *The Catherine Tate Show* to a natural close must have made her think even more deeply about motherhood. *The Bad Mother's Handbook* was an excellent ITV1 drama in which she played Karen Cooper, the mother of a pregnant teenage daughter Charlie (Holly Grainger) and the daughter of a woman suffering from dementia (Anne Reid). Grainger was a talented young actress who had previous appeared as Megan Boothe in ITV's long-running Sunday night saga *Where The Heart Is*. The drama, based on a best-selling novel by Kate Long, looked at the meaning of motherhood in all its different aspects. Having had her daughter very young, Karen now pins all her frustrated ambitions on Charlie. And, after applying for a passport for the first time, she sees her birth certificate and realizes she was adopted.

As Tate describes Karen: 'Her life has been one of compromise. She had great plans but has been left feeling that all the good things ended when she became pregnant at the age of sixteen. She couldn't go to university or get a job, she couldn't better her life. She's sharp with her mum and very cold when her daughter Charlie tells her she's pregnant. She can't believe her daughter has made the same mistake.' She said that loving the original novel and finding out that Anne Reid was going to play her mother convinced her to take the role.

Beautifully written and acted, the drama demonstrates all the joys and frustrations that come with being a parent. And Karen's journey, from being an unhappy, whining, reluctant mother and daughter, to realizing the depths of her love, is a particularly moving one.

One speech that she delivers to Charlie just after her daughter has given birth must have been particularly poignant. Trying to make up for how horrible she has been to Charlie while she was pregnant, Karen describes how it felt after she'd given birth to her. 'When you were born they handed you over and that was the first time I realized you were an actual person. And you fixed me with this stare as if to say you're mine, don't even think about giving me away. Because what you need to realize is that, as soon as I held you, I was bowled over, knocked flat by the way I felt like I'd do anything for you, like I knew what my life was for.'

The huge difference between this beautiful and traditional view of how the birth of a child affects its mother and what Tate went through personally cannot have been lost on her. That she made it so wholly believable is again testimony to her strength as an actress. The casting director deserves a huge pat on the back for this production too, as Anne Reid is unbearably moving as the gran who is losing it, while Holly Grainger is fresh, feisty and compelling as the teenage daughter. All in all, *The Bad Mother's Handbook* was another great career choice for Catherine Tate and won just over six million viewers, roughly one quarter of the available audience.

*

While Tate's relationship with Twig Clark appears as strong as ever, there are unlikely to be wedding bells. When asked about the possibility of marriage, Tate has always knocked the prospect down flat.

'I've never felt the need to get married, and having Erin hasn't changed that. I've probably got a deep-rooted fear of commitment, although having a child together is the biggest commitment you can make.'

If that weren't clear enough, she underlined the point after her star turn in the *Doctor Who* Christmas episode in 2006: 'I've just played a runaway bride in *Doctor Who* and wearing a wedding dress for five weeks is enough to knock anyone's enthusiasm for marriage.'

Even if she did decide to tie the knot, it would be no doubt with the minimum of fuss and with absolute privacy. There is no chance of anyone seeing the notoriously private Ms Tate's wedding pictures in *OK!* magazine, or anywhere else for that matter. She is even upset with herself for ever having mentioned daughter Erin in interviews: 'In the past, I've had photographers trying to snap her in our house, and the more I'm drawn to talk about her, the more vulnerable she becomes. Unfortunately, I wasn't given this advice early on, and talked about her quite happily. But had I known *The Catherine Tate Show* was going to become so popular, I would definitely have kept my mouth shut to preserve her privacy.'

CHAPTER EIGHT

Fame and Shyness

While she had spent most of her adult life striving to make it in a very public arena, fame, when it came, did not sit easy with Catherine Tate. In early interviews, around the time when her first BBC sitcom *Wild West* was coming out, she talked easily and funnily about her pregnancy, her life with partner Twig Clark and her dreams for the future. Even when *The Catherine Tate Show* was being launched, she seemed to have no fears of sharing her thoughts with interviewers and with the nation. But, as the show became a success, and interest understandably became greater, the enormity of being a public figure seemed to hit her. She became more closed about her life, gave fewer and less frank interviews, and seemed to want to shun the whole 'celebrity' tag. Caught in the trap of not being able to be successful without at least something being known about her private life, Tate shut down as much as she could.

Having admitted to being a 'painfully shy' child, it's no wonder that any level of public scrutiny would send her scuttling for cover. Her postnatal depression, which she suffered throughout the first two series of *The Catherine Tate Show*, can't have helped either. When you're feeling at rock bottom on a personal level, the last thing you'd need would be people wanting to find out about your inner thoughts. Being scrutinized for what you're wearing and how you're looking must have felt like some kind of fresh hell too.

Tate admitted recently that she lives in fear of appearing in a celebrity magazine dedicated to rooting out celebrities' weak spots. When asked about the intrusion of paparazzi into her life, she told *The Observer*: 'Oh, I don't think I'm high currency. If I'm in the line of pappery, they'll have a go, that's it. Though I do live in fear of being in the circle of shame in *Heat*, where they put a red ring around one of your toes and write, "Ugh! Mutant feet!" Or round your top lip with "Ugh! Rash from facial bleach!"'

She has seemed touchingly astonished that members of the public even know who she is, telling the *Radio Times* back in 2006: 'It never ceases to amaze me that people know who I am. I've just been filming *Doctor Who* in Wales, and somehow I just thought, "I'm in Wales. It's only people in London who know who I am. If that." And yet people kept coming up to me, saying (in a Welsh accent), "Am I bovvered?"'

There would seem to be a certain amount of denial in this attitude. Had she stopped to examine her viewing figures for the sketch show, which were into the millions, and her high profile appearances on *Comic Relief* and the Royal Variety Performance, then she would surely have known that she was a nationally recognizable figure.

Having laboured in the wilderness for the best part of fifteen years, there must be a small part of her that can now enjoy being so well known. She seemed to be more accepting of this in 2005, when her career was really beginning to hit new heights. '2005 has definitely been a great year,' she said. 'I don't want to say that it's been the pinnacle of my career because I don't want to jinx it, but I'm thrilled things have really taken off. I heard someone say, "Am I bovvered?" on *Coronation Street* the other day and I was like, "Oh, my God!" And I couldn't believe it when Kylie said she liked me.'

A greetings card with the *Mona Lisa* on it that her mother Josephine brought to her attention also forced her to reflect on just how ubiquitous she was becoming: 'There was a speech bubble coming out of the *Mona Lisa*, saying, "Am I bovvered?" and at the bottom it said, "The *Mona Lisa*, on show at the Catherine Tate Modern." I mean, oh my God, it was so bizarre.'

Her reactions to awards ceremonies and public events also say a lot about her ambivalent attitude to fame. When she was nominated for a Variety Club award in 2005, she took her glammed-up mother along as her date for the evening. In a last-minute panic though, she made the taxi driver take them to the back door of the Hilton on Park Lane, thus avoiding the red carpet and the photographers. Having hordes of people yelling at you and taking your photograph would be upsetting to all but the most hardened celebrity so her reaction was understandable. These are high profile, long-standing awards, designed to reward outstanding talent in entertainment and thus a big deal. Other winners that year included Stephen Fry, Simon Cowell, Gordon Ramsay and Imelda Staunton, so she was in excellent company. Mum Josephine was understandably miffed at missing this chance in the spotlight with her famous daughter. Said Tate later: 'My mum made it clear she wanted to go in the front.' And she has said of awards shows generally: 'I dread them. To be nominated is nice, but awards don't really matter to me. I'm really pleased I'm doing well because I can see how happy it's made my mum.'

This attitude to public attention is both understandable and endearing, though, and it's refreshing to see a famous figure who's neither a size zero nor desperate for their five minutes in the limelight.

While most female celebrities will call up the latest hot designers and borrow a fabulous frock for high-profile events, Tate took a very different route for her appearance at the British Academy of Film and Television Awards (BAFTAs). Just like the rest of us when faced with a glamorous event, she popped down to a make-up counter at a local department store and got one of the sales people to do her face. She did do them the courtesy of buying all the make-up though. Next stop? A trip to high street retailer Monsoon to pick up a spangly top. And hey presto, a more glitzed-up version of the Catherine Tate we all know and love, without resort to any professional pamperers. 'Well, if you borrow something, you feel obliged to go out there on the red carpet and get photographed, don't you? And that's not my thing at all. The other reason is that if I did call up and ask if they'd got anything in a size fourteen, I know what they'd say: "Would you like a bag instead?"' Tate means a designer handbag but you can almost hear her self-deprecating thought processes joking that a paper bag over her head might have made her more comfortable.

Her reluctance to be photographed extends to publicity shoots for interviews and to promote her latest projects, a necessary part of the life of any celebrity who wants to continue on their chosen career path. She confided to a *Times* journalist who was interviewing her in a photographer's studio: 'I thought on the way here what if the taxi had a tiny accident, a little bump? Then I would be a witness, you see, and have to miss the photo shoot.' This aversion to publicity can't be healthy for someone who needs it for their livelihood, and it's obviously an inner struggle that she goes through.

She has admitted to being plagued by negativity but that it's a hard habit to break as she's superstitious, and believes that if she starts to enjoy herself things will begin to go wrong. But she has coping mechanisms that enable her to turn her worst moments into material for her shows. 'I'm a very negative person, maybe a bit manic. But one thing that gets you through even the darkest hour is a tiny voice that puts it through a filter, and turns it out as a sketch at the other end. In any situation – awful, good or average – there's always part of me thinking, "That would be a good two-shot there."'

She has obviously thought long and hard about how to present her personality to the world at large, and admits that at all times she is controlling what people see of her. This sounds like it would be a fairly exhausting process, and it's little wonder that she has spoken of high anxiety levels in the past. She has taken what she learned at school – that by shielding herself with humour she could blend in – and carried it forward into adult, and public, life. In 2006 Catherine told a female *Observer* journalist: 'I realized that if you get yourself labelled as the funny one, people don't look any further. I've used that as I've got older. It's controlling: I decide what part of my personality you're seeing. I make the decisions on your behalf. I don't want you to look at me, I really don't. I don't want you to comment on my clothes, or my hair, or the way I look.'

While we all do this to a certain extent throughout the course of our daily lives, it seems fairly extreme to have analysed this trait to that level of preciseness. This is one woman who really doesn't want random strangers knowing her true self.

Her level of self-knowledge is impressive though, and it is this that must help her to be such an accurate observer of human nature. Her character creations are notable for their toe-curling accuracy, not least Paul and Sam, the Essex couple who crack themselves up with their own (lack of) wit. They provide probably the least funny of Tate's sketches though, most likely because their behaviour is the closest to the bone and the most uncomfortable.

It's no surprise that Tate's need for control and perfectionism also extends to her writing. 'I am far too much of a control freak. The mark of a brilliant writer is someone who gives you a script, and then listens to your ideas and takes them on board. I give someone my script and if they go, "Shall I say 'and' instead of 'but'," I just say no because suddenly I can feel my temperature rising. It's an insecurity thing really and an arrogance, perhaps. But with writing, if you're too open to everyone else's ideas, you can lose your own voice.'

Despite her huge and obvious success, there's a part of

Catherine Tate that still sees herself as someone waiting for the phone to ring. It's as if she won't allow herself to enjoy the good things that are happening, for fear they will be taken away again. 'I still think of myself as a jobbing actor – you never really shake that off from the wilderness years. You never forget that you're only as good as your last job and your next job.'

It's why she's kept herself so busy over the last few years, running from one project to the next without giving herself time to take a breath. She admits that she finds it hard to turn work down: 'I've gone from one job to another with no breaks in the past few years. It's all been a bit manic. I don't want to work myself into the ground – or hit the bottle in five years after being teetotal my whole life...'

*

A vegetarian, Tate has never drunk alcohol, smoked cigarettes, taken drugs, or sunbathed. This would explain her beautiful skin, of which certain interviewers have gone into raptures of description at its 'luminescence'. To be teetotal in today's society is unusual, to say the least, and this rejection of all mind-altering substances would seem to fit in with the idea of wanting to be very much in control of everything. After describing to a *Guardian* interviewer how tight a rein she keeps on her work, she was asked if that applied in her private life too: 'Well, I don't drink, smoke or do drugs and I think that comes from the same place. I think it's something to do with the fear that if I do them, I won't be myself.'

She has said that her only weakness is food, of which she is inordinately fond, and that, for kicks, she eats. She claimed that her guiltiest pleasure is Coke floats, glasses of Coke with ice cream floated in them – 'About four a day' – and she once went into raptures when describing a food shop she stumbled into on a visit to New York. 'I went into a grocery shop in New York once. Just an ordinary shop. And. It had. A wall. Of yoghurts. I couldn't have legislated for it in my head. I could feel my heart racing. And that's just yoghurt! Healthy! Although knowing the Americans, it's probably got cake added to it or something. God knows what I'd be like in an ice cream parlour! I can't go back to the US until I'm dangerously thin.'

It's nice to know she has one weakness at least and that it's something as harmless as food. The extras on the DVD of her 2007 Christmas special include shots of intense script meetings and, scattered across the table, are piles of fruit, cartons of salad, and stray M&S food bags. After all, who can work properly without recourse to the best our finest grocer has to offer?

Ever self-critical, Tate also claims to be a lazy person, though it's hard to find evidence of that in her workload of the past few years. There can have been precious little time to sit around with her feet up between three TV series of her own, four films, a couple of TV dramas, a whole series of *Doctor Who*, and two stage plays. 'But I hesitate to call myself a control freak,' she has said, 'because if I am I manage to combine it with being desperately lazy. That's just the worst kind to be. Because it's only to go my way, but I can't be bothered to make it happen. But I'm really not ambitious and I actually think I'm lax about my career. There are certain things I couldn't care less about. I can be a right lazy cow.'

The Brunswick Centre in Bloomsbury, London, is a familiar sight to Catherine as it is where she was brought up.

At the British Comedy Awards in 2004, Catherine receives the 'Best Comedy Newcomer' trophy flanked by Jimmy Carr and Ronni Ancona.

Catherine as Mitzi Kosinski in the Agatha Christie ITV drama *Marple: A Murder Is Announced* in 2005.

Lauren, the truculent teenager whose 'Am I bovvered?' catchphrase became part of everyday language all over the UK.

Above: Lauren meets the Queen at the Royal Variety Performance at the Millennium Centre in Cardiff in November 2005, in the company of Welsh singers Katherine Jenkins and Charlotte Church.

Lauren appeared on this poster at the British Comedy Awards in London in December 2005.

Above: Catherine on stage at the Gielgud Theatre in London with *Friends* star David Schwimmer in *Some Girls* in 2005.

A slight injury left Catherine having to use a crutch as she took to the red carpet for the 2006 BAFTA ceremony along with Ricky Gervais and his girlfriend Jane Fallon.

Filming 'The Runaway Bride' *Dr Who* Christmas special in Cardiff with David Tennant in July 2006.

Catherine appeared in the 2006 movie *Love and Other Disasters* along with, clockwise from foreground left: Brittany Murphy, Santiago Cabrera, Elliot Cowan and Matthew Rhys.

Catherine as Aunt Lila in the 2006 movie *Sixty Six* about a boy's Bar Mitzvah clashing with the 1966 World Cup Final.

Catherine with Holly Grainger as Karen and Charlie Cooper in the 2007 TV special *The Bad Mother's Handbook*, based on the novel by Kate Long.

Catherine posing with Dawn French and Sophia Myles at London's Mayfair Hotel for the gala screening to launch the new *Dr Who* series in March 2007.

David Tennant, John Barrowman and Catherine visited Capital Radio in London, bringing their own brand of mayhem to the station's breakfast show while promoting *Dr Who* in April 2008.

Catherine attended the BAFTA ceremony at the London Palladium in May 2007, narrowly missing out on the award for 'Best Comedy Programme or Series'.

If she really is as lazy as she makes out then she's doing a stunning job of disguising it, and her career is doing fine without any self-propulsion. She claimed in 2006 that she'd be happy if her career ended tomorrow, and that she'd follow her alternative dream of being an astrologer. She has said that she believes in the trends in the sky and is a big admirer of Jonathan Cainer, one of Britain's best paid and most sought after astrologers. Academic Richard Dawkins, professor of the public understanding of science at Oxford University, may have branded him a charlatan but Tate, and millions of others, believe in his predictions. In fact, if the acting and writing work dried up, astrology is where her future lies: 'I would have trained to be one before but there aren't any courses.'

Born on May 12, Catherine Tate is a Taurus and this following description of that star sign would certainly seem to bear out her faith in the stars. 'Underneath their cool, calm and collected exterior, Taureans differ greatly from all the other signs of the zodiac. Taureans manage to discreetly stay apart from the crowd, even if they have a well-earned reputation for being socialisers. They will let others get close, but only so close as they want them. Some claim that trying to get your point across to a Taurean, should they not want to hear you, is rather similar to talking to the trees – they simply won't budge. And, there is no such thing as an open-book Taurean. Their feelings, fears and desires often run far deeper than anyone around them would guess. Like the butterfly that chooses to remain hidden in its cocoon until it is ready and prepared to emerge, so the true Taurean spirit remains hidden behind a veneer of day-to-day activities.'

This description, taken from the *Psychic Guild* website, would certainly seem to square with her descriptions of herself. Choosing only to reveal what she wants of her personality, being reluctant to take on board suggestions about her work, and generally keeping herself to herself, all fit with the Taurean personality.

Tate has also talked openly about her fear of commitment. As recently as 2005, she still hadn't bought a house, not wanting to give herself a mortgage. 'I still rent a house, and will continue to rent until I can buy a house outright. I have a deep-seated fear of commitment. Marriage has never been in my game plan. But we're very committed to each other and Twig is such a lovely man. We're really happy together.'

This would seem to go back to her fear of believing that everything is really going well, at the risk of jinxing it. One interviewer suggested that she must have realised how well she was doing as she headed into Number Ten Downing Street to record a sketch with the then Prime Minister Tony Blair. But she says not. 'No, I don't really reflect on things, and I certainly don't go home and talk about it. My main memory of the day was, "Ooh, we've not quite written the script yet." The thing is, I'm very much a bottle half-empty person.'

She seems to cling to her negativity like a life raft: 'It's like that thing, if it ain't broke, don't fix it. And I think I've not done too badly being negative – because I never had this drive to be successful. But then I think I maybe did...'

One peculiar and quite sweet thing that has changed her outlook somewhat was acquiring a cat for her daughter Erin. Having previously stated that 'I don't like cats with their little cat heads,' she seems to have executed a spectacular *volte-face*. 'This cat has changed my life, this cat is why I'm giving up my "it's cool to be negative" attitude because I cannot be negative round this cat. I love this cat. I just love him.'

She also talked about the said cat at some length on *Friday Night With Jonathan Ross*. As big as *Parkinson* was in its heyday, Ross's chat show is now a national institution, attracting the most high profile of guests and very healthy ratings. Its star is one of the BBC's most highly paid presenters and to appear on it is deemed both an honour and a career boost. 'I've got a cat and I think he's the reason I haven't had another baby because he's my ginger son,' she told an amused Ross. 'And I'm convinced he's gay too. He lets me cradle him like a baby.' She goes on to describe how she got him from Battersea Dogs' Home (which also houses and looks for homes for cats), and how the woman rang up to tell her there was a problem with this particular cat, and the 'problem' was that he was ginger. 'As true as God! The discrimination of my people goes down to the animal kingdom. I said, "That's mighty fine, lady, because we're a ginger household."'

While she has gone as far as admitting that she's done OK, in the grand scheme of things, Tate seems reluctant to take it very seriously. Back in 2006 she joked: 'I think I've done alright. Mainly because I'd have been a bitter, miserable failure. So it's just as well that I didn't fail really!' But she is adamant that she will never be seduced by the trappings of celebrity and that she will certainly never be seen gracing the pages of *Hello!* or *OK!* magazines. In fact, her image is rarely in the newspapers, unless it's a shot of her filming something or shyly clutching an award. She has said very sternly: 'I refuse to get caught up in my so-called celebrity. It doesn't even register on my radar. Yes, people recognize me and talk to me about their favourite characters from the sketch show but I never read the papers. Even my friends and family know better than to mention anything they've read about me. It's simply off-limits.'

If this makes her sound a little po-faced then it's probably misleading, as she's surrounded by close friends and family and is as funny and warm in real life as she can be on screen. But she admits that she can be a hard nut to crack, and going up to her on the street and trying to be her new best friend probably isn't a winning strategy. 'Yes, I think people would say I'm a difficult person to get to know. But that's because I don't come up and go, "Hiiiiiiyyyyyyaaaa, love your shirrrrrt!"'And while she enjoys life and wrings as much pleasure out of it as she can, she seems to have a morbid fear of unnaturally happy people. 'I do think if you've not spent most of your day having a really good laugh, it's a shame. Look, what I'm not is a cheery person. I find cheeriness quite exhausting. I find cheery people too much... they have no negative filter or sarcastic filter or dark filter. You can sniff it out. It's like a club they want you to join, do you know what I mean?' she asked an interviewer from *The Guardian*. 'I'm not a great hugger, either. Don't force me to hug people. People I like I will, but please, I don't know you, don't hug me!'

She is also horrified at the idea that she might lapse into her famous characters with her real friends: 'I think it would be awful to be anything other than what I am. With my friends it would be absolutely intolerable if I came in and went, "I hate these trousers, but am I bovvered though?" Awful.'

Her combination of superstition and negativity certainly seems to have served her well in her career and life so far. The carping about her casting as *Doctor Who*'s assistant and the odd critical comment about her comedy aside, she's had quite a smooth ride from the press. Her strategy for avoiding the limelight as much as possible seems to be working. Other celebrities who moan about press intrusion but turn up semi-clad to the opening of an envelope could probably learn a few lessons from her. And despite her obvious softening over her beloved ginger cat, she isn't planning on changing her winning formula.

'I'm never going to lose my negativity – I wouldn't like to. I do think that those really, really cheerful people are probably manic depressives. Or murderers.'

CHAPTER NINE

Catchphrases

It seems that it's been impossible to open a newspaper in the last few years without having a headline scream out at you with some variation on the theme of 'Am I bovvered?' When Catherine Tate first uttered this line on national television, in the very first episode of her sketch show, she could have had no idea of its massive impact on society.

Stroppy teen Lauren's defensive retort has been adopted by truculent schoolchildren, newspaper subeditors and office workers alike, becoming an instantly recognizable catchphrase. A variation of it ('Is one bovvered?') has been directed at the Queen herself, while a prime minister in office borrowed it to make a point on *Comic Relief*, and maybe buy himself back some credibility into the bargain.

The irony is that Tate claims never to have set out to create such a catchphrase, and that it merely developed naturally from Lauren's, shall we say, attitudinal problems. It was when trying out material for the first series of her show at the Latchmere Theatre in south-west London that she first realized its possible impact. As everyone roared with laughter at its repetition, so she threw the line in more and more, only to reap even greater audience response. Some would say that tiny audience in a room above a pub in Battersea have a lot to answer for. 'Bovvered', while becoming widely familiar, has also been a source of great irritation, sometimes even to its creator herself.

Tate seems genuinely bewildered at how this one phrase has spread like wildfire throughout the country, and how it will most certainly haunt her to her dying day. 'That one actually happened by accident,' she explained. 'I never expected people to repeat it. If you analyse it, a catchphrase is just something that people say in normal speech – people often say they're not bothered about things.' Well, they certainly do now, changing the 'th' to a double 'v' and demonstrating that they're down with the current parlance.

We all of us like to latch on to something that gives us common ground with others. Like watching soap operas and discussing the different characters and plots, catchphrases can act like social cement. If you can say 'How very dare you!' to someone in fun and see the glint of recognition in their eyes, you know you've made a connection. And they don't really have to make sense – from 'Ooh Betty' in 1970s sitcom *Some Mothers Do 'Ave 'Em* to 'Don't panic!' from *Dad's Army* and 'It's goodnight from him' in *The Two Ronnies*, anything comforting and familiar can make us feel connected.

'Bovvered' was even named Word Of The Year in 2006 by the compilers of the Oxford English Dictionary. It reached their august attention after Susie Dent from Channel 4's *Countdown* included it in her essay *The Language Report*, which was designed to high-light emerging vocabulary. Dent, a lexicographer, is the resident dictionary expert on the popular words and numbers game, the first show ever to be broadcast on Channel 4. Other words on her list included: WAGs (wives and girlfriends), 'waparazzi' (ordinary people snapping celebrities on their mobile phones), 'offlish' (business jargon), and 'Anna Kournikova', a poker expression describing an Ace and a King, and so-called because it seems like a good hand but rarely wins anything. Kournikova had a lot of success with doubles tennis but failed to make it to the finals of any major Grand Slam tournaments playing solo. She must have been delighted at her inclusion in gambling slang.

Dent said at the time: 'Bovvered neatly reflects our culture and its linguistic influences. It is also arguably an extension of "chav" which caused something of a stir when it was named Word Of The Year in 2004. Both words illustrate the power of language to divide opinion and excite debate by evoking a whole social milieu. The key difference is in their register – while one is a derogatory label, the other is a TV comic's catchphrase which has caught the public imagination and packs its punch differently, as a summary of a mindset recognizable to most of us.'

A spokesman from the OED added: '"Am I bovvered?" had already come to be seen as the perfect expression of a generation of teenagers and their speaking style. Now in 2006 "bovvered" has taken over from "whatever" as the signature phrase of teenagers, and to challenge the *Little Britain* catchphrase "yeah-but-no-but-yeah" as the embodiment of couldn't-care-less adolescence.'

Blimey. For a throwaway line in a TV sketch show, it's certainly become the centre of some heated intellectual debate and analysis. Tate must surely have had her moments of incredulity as this highbrow tableau unfolded before her. She told *The Daily Telegraph* the following year, in a lovely demonstration of under-statement: 'It's a bit weird, this whole "Am I bovvered?" thing. I mean, I could have asked for no greater response to my show than for people to quote it back at me in the street. But I never went out to make a catchphrase.'

But it wasn't just Lauren's 'Face? Bovvered?' that caught the public's imagination. Many of us picked up on the filth that came out of character Nan's mouth at the exact moment of mental mood swing, adopting 'What a fucking liberty!' as a handy way of injecting some humour into a situation.

Again, Tate professes herself bewildered at how this entered the national consciousness. 'It's completely weird the way people pick up on certain aspects. I didn't write each character to have a catchphrase. I mean, with Lauren there was a conscious thing for her to say, "Am I bovvered?" every time she appeared, just as a teenage trait, but with the old woman and "What a fuckin' liberty!" – that passed me by. Then, when we were filming the series, I said it and it got a huge round of applause! And now it's a repetitive slogan you hear when you knock over your orange squash.'

While Lauren never swore, as Tate was very sensitive to the fact that she was a teenager and a schoolgirl, Nan was somehow able to get away with the filthiest of language, leaving the vast majority of us laughing our heads off. Tate attributes this to the privilege of old age and the fact that old people swearing is simply intrinsically funny.

Lest we forget the hugely entertaining and camper than Christmas Derek Faye, his oft-repeated 'How very dare you!' is frequently heard wherever you go. As well as the appropriateness of this phrase in a variety of situations, it is also its cadence that is so appealing. This ability to bring a smile to someone's face with the use of a simple phrase is a testament to both Tate's talent and her uncanny ear for normal speech. Geordie Georgie, the incorrigible fundraiser for lost causes in the north-east of England, also made a bit of an impact with her 'laugh it up!', a line also heard if someone wants to invoke Tate's humour.

*

Catchphrases, if they are to catch on, can never usually be inserted cynically into our lexicon though. We can usually smell a rat if someone is trying desperately to get us to adopt some word or phrase. Tate herself agrees with this: 'I've always thought you can see it a mile off when writers try to do that. I have never tried to manufacture catchphrases. I've certainly never put any pressure on myself to come up with them – partly because I don't think I could top "Am I bovvered?"'

She cites 'It's Chico time', the catchphrase invented and pushed by 2005 *X Factor* contestant Chico, as an example of something the public wouldn't accept. Otherwise known as Yousseph Slimani, Chico was a former mountain goat herder born in Britain but who grew up in Morocco. He pushed 'It's Chico time' as his own catchphrase, attempting to use it to keep himself in the public consciousness. 'It's strange because you can't actually write a catchphrase, you can't make people repeat something. It's people that make it a catchphrase, which is why I think "It's Chico time" didn't quite catch on, because it was being told to us that this was a catchphrase.'

Mind you, Chico's single of the same name did reach number one in the UK singles charts in March of 2006. Here was a man who knew that if you hammered something home hard enough, it was bound to stick with someone.

Another show that was hugely successful in putting words into people's mouths was *Little Britain*. David Walliams and Matt Lucas's runaway success of a sketch show gave us 'Yeah, but no, but yeah', 'the only gay in the village', 'we're laydees', 'computer says no', and 'I want that one!' to name but a few. Tate, who had worked with Lucas on the stand-up comedy circuit, admits that she herself uses their catchphrases in everyday life: 'I mean, I can't say I want something now without going, "I want that one!" or "Yeah, but no, but." You can't stop yourself because it's already in there. You certainly can't write the catchphrase before you create the character.'

*

Given the simultaneous success of *The Catherine Tate Show* and *Little Britain*, there was bound to be a backlash against the cult of the catchphrase and so it was. Writing in *The Daily Telegraph*, TV critic Alex Mitchell criticized comics' over-reliance on the familiar to make us laugh. On catchphrases she said: 'We seem to be living in a golden age for them, a time when no sketch show is complete unless you've heard at least half the words in it before. Are we so imbecilic that we must recognize what we're hearing to find it funny, like Pavlov's dogs, jerked into laughter by familiar phrases?' She singled out Lauren as being a particularly bad repeat offender: 'As for Lauren, yes, she was funny the first four times but any humour in her character has now been lost, buried under a predictable skip-full of catchphrases.'

Interestingly, Ricky Gervais and Stephen Merchant's *Extras*, that went out in a double bill with *The Catherine Tate Show*, also took a pot-shot at the cult of catchphrases. The naturalistic comedy that looked at the life of a former extra in TV and films, who had made it to become a star, was praised to the skies by the critics. Gervais had been unable to put a foot wrong since *The Office* became a cult, critical and ratings success, and it reflected well on Tate that her show was being bracketed with his in a high-profile time slot. Gervais's character in *Extras*, Andy Millman, an actor in a dire sitcom, constantly overused the phrase 'Are you having a laugh?' in a bid for popularity. Lauded for the subtlety of his comedy in creations such as *The Office*, Gervais obviously thought he was in a good position to level some cheeky criticism at the other strands of comedy that had caught our collective imaginations in a more straightforward manner.

It wasn't just highbrow journalists and comedians who were tiring of high-profile catchphrases, however. Office workers constantly being bombarded with a hail of 'Am I bovvered?'s also started to object. When recruitment firm Office Angels conducted a survey on workplace jargon, 'Am I bovvered?' emerged as the most annoying phrase being bandied about. Some forty-two per cent of the 1,600 people surveyed said that they would like to see this particular catchphrase banned from the office environment. Listed along with it in the category of jargon *faux-pas* were 'blue sky thinking', 'singing from the same hymn sheet' and 'There's no "I" in team'.

All this is fair enough but when you consider the same survey came up with the following as 'cool office buzz-phrases', you have to wonder: 'thought grenade' (apparently shorthand for explosively good ideas), 'Let's sunset that' (bad ideas that are never mentioned again), 'Little "r" me' (a request for a private answer to an email), and 'information touchpoint' (something to replace an old-fashioned meeting). They make 'Am I bovvered?' look positively elegant – at least Tate's catchphrase makes sense. Eighty-three per cent of those surveyed admitted condemning colleagues for using out-of-date terms so you obviously have to keep up to date with jargon, however ungrammatical and ugly, to survive in today's office world.

Broadsheet newspapers, those arbiters of good taste, also started adopting variations of 'bovvered' in headlines, often in stories bearing no relation to Catherine Tate, her comedy show, or the character of Lauren Cooper. Tate, still clearly reeling from the Bovvered phenomenon, said in 2006: 'It's crazy, there was even a piece in a Sunday broadsheet about *Mrs Ratcliffe's Revolution* [a British film in which she starred], and the headline was "Proletariat Utopia – Am I Bovvered?". It's especially weird when I see it being used in news stories that are nothing to do with me. There was something about Gordon Brown not being bovvered the other day, and that was in a posh paper too. I wonder if I will ever be able to escape it.'

If some of the great British public were tiring of being asked 'Am I bovvered?', a certain church group wasn't, and decided to capitalise on the catchphrase's popularity. Christian Publishing and Outreach (CPO), the UK's leading religious publicity supplier, used this phrase along with 'How very dare you!' and *Little Britain*'s 'Yeah, but no, but yeah', made famous by shell-suited Vicki Pollard, and the same show's Andy Pipkin's 'Yeah, I know.'

Using the phrases on a series of brightly coloured posters designed to attract young people into the church, they then put biblical quotations underneath. In the case of 'Yeah, but no, but yeah', it was followed by the words of Peter the Apostle: 'Always be prepared to give an answer to everyone who asks you to give the reason for the hope that you have.'

The sets of posters were being sold to individual churches for £25. Representatives of Tate, as well as Lucas and Walliams, threatened legal action, claiming that using their most famous lines on posters breached their intellectual property rights. At the time, a spokesman from the CPO admitted that permission to use the catchphrases had not been sought and the posters were withdrawn.

As both Tate and the men behind *Little Britain* have often been accused of encouraging bad behaviour in teens through the antics of their anti-social characters Lauren and Vicki Pollard, it was peculiar, to say the least, that a religious organization should seek to use their work in order to recruit youngsters to Christianity. But, legal issues aside, perhaps the move wasn't as daft as it seemed. Catchphrases from both shows had been identified as being the most popular in schools, often driving teachers to distraction. 'Am I bovvered?' joined 'Whatever!', 'D'oh! (from *The Simpsons*), 'Innit' and 'The computer says no' (*Little Britain*), 'You are the weakest link. Goodbye!' (*The Weakest Link*), and 'You have been evicted' (*Big Brother*) in the top ten phrases teachers reported hearing most of in school.

When asked about this, Tate seemed embarrassed that her work had been hijacked in quite such a negative way: 'Oh my God, I get letters from teachers saying they really like my show, but can I please kill off that character? [Lauren] They say, "She's making our lives a misery." Kids just chant it in the classroom. Well, OK, but I never pitched my show to a pre-teen audience. But once the kids get hold of it, that's what gives it a longer life. It's one thing me dressing up and doing Lauren and certain people repeating it, but having pre-adolescent kids who are a bit lairy anyway saying it to you, I think it's a bit scary myself!'

It must be pretty amazing to realize that something you coined has gone on not only to enter the Oxford English Dictionary and be the subject of intellectual debate and national headlines, but also be common slang and shorthand that sums up an entire generation. Tate has said: 'The "bovvered" thing really did take on a life of its own. I must admit I do find it all rather over-whelming sometimes, but I can't subvert it – that would be churlish anyway.' And in typical Tate fashion, she says that she tries to avoid thinking about it or focusing on it too much: 'It's not like I walk on the street thinking, "I'm the person who says, 'Am I bovvered?'" When I finish a show I don't think about it, I lie in bed watching DVDs of *Sex And The City*.' Now, if Sarah

Jessica Parker started accusing Miranda, Samantha and Charlotte of disrespecting her and calling her mum a Pikey and her dad a wino, she really would have to start worrying. These cosmopolitan, glossy characters in the worldwide hit that examined the lives of sexually liberated women are a galaxy away from the awkward, insecure creations of Tate's fevered imagination. No wonder she likes to relax with them.

Of course, there is always money to be made when catchphrases become so universally popular. As the show took off, unofficial Catherine Tate character merchandise began to spring up like weeds. 'Am I bovvered?' was emblazoned across T-shirts, mugs and anything that would carry a three-word slogan, while greetings cards, posters and other memorabilia abounded. Initially reluctant to sanction any official merchandise, probably for fear of looking like she was cashing in too readily on her comic creations, Tate was eventually persuaded that it was the way forward. It was announced in 2005 that a range of merchandise would be launched, all with Tate's approval. An insider told the *Daily Mirror*: 'It's at a very early stage, but Catherine will decide what is made. She is heavily involved in the process.'

The company tasked with translating Nan, Lauren and Derek into easily sellable comedy products was Granada Ventures. They had also been behind *Little Britain*'s range of talking dolls, T-shirts, mugs and puzzles which were rumoured to have racked up some £50 million in sales, netting Walliams and Lucas £6 million between them. It was understandable, then, that boss of Granada Ventures Gerry Donohoe said at the time: 'We are delighted to be working with a creative genius like Catherine.'

Tate was being interviewed by a journalist from *The Observer* when she looked at a prototype for a talking mug. Depending on how you put it down, it either sang out 'Am I bovvered?', 'How very dare you!' or 'What a liberty!' (They'd presumably edited out the 'f' word to make it more suitable for a family market.) After looking at the mug, Tate said: 'The problem is there's so much unofficial stuff out there already and with this, they give some of the profits to charity, so they make it hard for you to say no. It's damage limitation and good causes, it's hard to resist.' She also released the full scripts from the first two series of *The Catherine Tate Show* under the title, *Am I Bovvered?* A slouching Lauren stares aggressively from the cover as she points at her face. Clearly not bovvered at all.

It's obvious that the immense popularity of the catchphrases of some of Tate's characters has been both a blessing and a curse. On the one hand, it brought notoriety, instant fame and money; on the other, it made people focus on one small part of her work. It's important to remember that many of the characters she portrayed in the show did not come with their own ready-made, easily absorbable jingle. Elaine Figgis, the bakery worker looking for love on the internet, was multi-layered and entirely without a catchphrase, as was Bunty, the oldest cheerleader in town, the Enigmatic Cop, and even Bernie, the nymphomaniac nurse. Although 'I don't kiss and tell, I shout and shag!' is a brilliant line, Bernie used it only once. It was her snorting, facial expressions and easy lust that we remember the best. (Ah, Bernie, we hope you're having a great ride, wherever you are.)

While keen to point out that she didn't want to seem ungrateful for her success, Tate was also intent on distancing herself somewhat from the catchphrase-spouting monsters she had created. As someone who had trained as a serious actress and had ambitions to work in television and theatre, she understandably didn't want to be associated with 'bovvered' always, only and forever.

The catchphrase mania is almost certainly what caused her to end the show after three series. She said in 2006: 'I instinctively feel that three series is enough. I don't want it to drag on, where you have a very old schoolgirl trotting out, "Am I bovvered?" If in five years' time the only thing that I've done that is remembered is a teenager saying, "Am I bovvered?" then I'd worry.'

So Lauren perished in an unfortunate kayaking accident, leaving behind her the headstone inscribed with 'I Still Ain't Bovvered', while Tate continues to distance herself from her insanely popular catchphrases with as much grace as she can muster.

CHAPTER TEN

Charity Performances

While her characters had become hugely popular throughout the course of her three series of *The Catherine Tate Show* and two Christmas specials, it was when Tate took them outside the confines of her specially created world that they really made their biggest impact. As first Lauren, then Nan, Geordie Georgie and Elaine Figgis made special appearances on *Comic Relief*, *Children In Need* or the Royal Variety Performance, they reached an even bigger, and probably more shocked, audience. Tabloid headlines and even greater popularity followed.

Pigtail-swinging Lauren was the first to break out of the television studio when she joined boy band McFly on stage for a special *Comic Relief* sketch in March, 2005. The hot boy band of the day, McFly at the time were attracting screaming teenage girl fans everywhere they went. Along with Liese and Ryan, Lauren joined a specially selected audience of school children all lined up to ask the boys their pre-prepared questions. Hosted by everyone's favourite smartarse Simon Amstell, now host of irreverent pop quiz *Never Mind The Buzzcocks*, the strand started innocently enough. It ran just like all those other carefully scripted sessions with famous stars that have been on the go since Noel Edmonds' *Multi Coloured Swap Shop* was the cutting edge in children's TV.

Amstell, who had started his career on children's channel Nickelodeon and gone on to co-present *Popworld* on Channel 4 with Miquita Oliver, was perfect as Lauren's secret co-conspirator. His sarcasm and biting sense of humour had made always made him a weird choice for children's television.

Girl number one asked the boys what was their favourite colour. Girl number two coyly asked whether they liked being famous. Then Lauren's sullen face came into focus and the nervous young lads were put on the spot with 'Why are you so rubbish?'

Clearly, they were in on the joke and had willingly set themselves up for a roasting from Britain's most famous teen. But it still made for uncomfortable viewing as it wasn't always obvious that they really knew what was going on, or whether their agent had sold them a pup by allowing them to get into this in the first place.

Amstell gently remonstrated with Lauren, telling her she'd been given a nicer question, but she insisted that he thought they were rubbish too. Many denials were eventually ended with an agreement that Amstell did think they were 'slightly rubbish'. Cue nervous laughter from the McFly boys. Insult was further added to injury when Lauren asked them if they were gutted that Charlie had left – a reference to rival boy band Busted who had recently lost one of their members. Amstell's assertion that the boys were

McFly and not Busted caused Lauren to launch into one of her trademark monologues that ended with 'But I ain't McBothered!' Ordered off the set for spoiling things, she then asked one of the band to sign her knee and flounced off with the parting shot: 'You can't even spell.'

Watching the clip again some three years later, it isn't vintage Lauren and doesn't reach the dizzy heights of cleverness that some of her sketches did. The one with the French oral exam springs to mind as a particularly fine example of Lauren at her funniest. In it she goes from her usual sullen truculence to responding to her exasperated French teacher in fluent French but with her usual catchphrases inserted. It demonstrated that Lauren wasn't stupid, something Tate was keen to prove at that point. But the McFly interview did bring both Lauren and Catherine Tate to a far wider audience, given the millions who tune in for Red Nose Day every other year. The main fund-raising event for *Comic Relief*, Red Nose Day sees people all over the country getting involved in sponsored silliness and buying plastic or foam red noses to wear during the day to show their support. It was later the same year, though, that Tate and her truculent alter ego were really to hit the big time.

So God bless the producers of the seventy-seventh annual Royal Variety Performance: as well as booking Shirley Bassey, Charlotte Church, Katherine Jenkins and Cliff Richard, they also saw fit to invite along the cheeky Catherine Tate trio of Lauren, Ryan and Liese. Held at the Wales Millennium Centre in Cardiff, it was attended by both Her Majesty the Queen and Prince Philip. Let's hope that Tate enjoyed her visit to the Welsh capital as she'd be spending a lot more time here when she signed on for *Doctor Who*. While the royal couple most probably enjoyed Cliff's medley of *Move It*, *The Young Ones* and *We Don't Talk Any More*, they were in for a shock when confronted with this horrible shower.

Wheeled on, slouched on wooden seats, Lauren, Ryan and Liese seemed blissfully unaware of where they were at first. 'What's this thing again?' asked a nonchalant Lauren. When told she'd be meeting the Queen, she pronounced the prospect 'boring', until Ryan begged to differ and she went along with his every word. After discussing host Sharon Osbourne, wife of rocker Ozzy Osbourne and talent show judge, as well as Lauren's prospects of winning next year's *X Factor* in which Osbourne is a deciding factor, they suddenly spotted Her Majesty. 'Don't make it obvious! Queen at two o'clock!' was followed by Ryan's admiring 'She is fierce' and a chorused trademark 'Aaal-riiiiight.' The next line, spoken by Liese, is the one that caused the most controversy as she observed: 'That old man sitting next to her has fallen asleep.' This got a hugely appreciative bellow from the galleries but apparently went down less well with the Duke of Edinburgh. But more of that later.

Another cracking line was Lauren's: 'Oh my God! What has she come as?' After a discussion of the Queen's jewellery, Lauren pronounces her 'well bing bing' and then has to take the shame for the mispronunciation. When Ryan informs her that the Queen is laughing at her, she starts haranguing the monarch with choice questions like 'Are you calling my dad a wino?' This culminated in her asking the Queen, 'Is one bovvered? Is one's face bovvered?', enquiring who was looking after the corgis and suggesting they all went to Balmoral. A call on Lauren's mobile then confirmed that she'd been made a Dame.

How Tate had the chutzpah to carry off this immensely cheeky skit is anyone's guess. The producers of what has traditionally been a very safe show of 'family entertainment' were taking a huge risk with a very daring performer. It has to be said that shots of the Queen during the performance would suggest that she was amused and that the beheading that Ryan was predicting was not on the cards. Tate did confide afterwards that she had had some reservations about such a high-risk strategy: 'When we were rehearsing I was saying, "Can I actually say to the Queen, 'Are you calling my mum a prostitute?'" But I think the general consensus was that we took it as far as we could in the name of comedy.'

She was also fairly certain that the Queen had got the joke and wasn't too enraged about it: 'Hmmm. I know the Queen was laughing. She definitely laughed when we said, "I think that old man next to her has fallen asleep." But I think it was a bit left field for them. Those three people coming out and talking really fast and saying, "Are you disrespecting me?" to the *Queen*... I think it might have been a bit of a culture shock.'

The tabloids were then alive with reports that an aide of Prince Philip's had complained to the producers during the show's interval that the sketch had gone too far. The powers that be behind the Royal Variety Performance were quick to deny this though, as Tate explained: 'It's been in the papers that Prince Philip complained, but he didn't – the Royal Variety Performance put out a statement. There was never any intention to offend or even to be controversial. Saying that, I think I sailed quite close to the wind...'

Prostitute? Wino? Corgis? 'My husband and I' in a high-pitched voice? Sailing close to the wind is another one of Tate's classic understatements. In the same month in 2005, she took on another *grande dame*, although this time a fictional one. For that year's *Children In Need*, Lauren entered the hallowed turf of Albert Square to square up to a bevy of *EastEnders*. We first see the normally hard as nails character of Stacey Slater (Lacey Turner) running into the Queen Vic pub to seek help from land-lady Peggy Mitchell (Barbara Windsor). Some scary bird from Up West thinks Stacey's stolen her boyfriend and is on the warpath.

'If she thinks she can turn up in Walford shouting the odds, she's got another think coming,' says a loyal Peggy. Cut to Lauren sauntering into the launderette to subject Little Mo (Kacey Ainsworth) to some hardcore questioning about Stacey's where-abouts. Two litres of fabric conditioner down Little Mo's throat later, Lauren finds her prey.

The meat of this sketch is the encounter between feisty Peggy Mitchell and the hardcore schoolgirl. Once these two set eyes upon each other, the disputed boyfriend isn't even mentioned. Recognizing a challenge when she sees one, Lauren launches into an offensive immediately. The escalating questions kick off with 'Are you a Cock-er-ney?' and graduate to 'Is it that you are a Cockney sparrow?', 'Do you eat jellied eels for your breakfast?', 'Are you doing the Lambeth Walk? Oy.', 'Do you know Chas and Dave?', 'Is it that you are Chas and Dave's mum?' to 'Did you abandon Chas and Dave?'

Tate gets in some choice digs at the long-running soap, including a crack about the fact that nobody in the Square owns a washing machine, the launderette having acted as a handy yet implausible meeting place to exchange gossip and develop storylines for more than two decades. Lauren eventually batters Peggy down to an exhausted wreck with her verbal barrage. As Terry Wogan, veteran host of both *Children In Need* and *The Eurovision Song Contest*, said when he introduced the sketch, it was: 'One of those moments that makes *Children In Need* truly unique. Britain's newest brightest comedy star joins up with one of the BBC's most popular shows.'

The great thing was that Catherine Tate, as with the Royal Variety Performance, wasn't afraid to take a few well-aimed pot shots at a British institution. This was Lauren at her most menacing and, as former colleague and *Father Ted* writer Arthur Mathews said, Tate's comedy is nothing if not 'ballsy'.

*

This description of Tate's comedy as 'ballsy' was to spring to mind again some eighteen months later when, in March 2007 Tate did an unprecedented five different sketches for *Comic Relief*. As with the Christmas special in which Lauren died, pre-publicity was again feverish and a DVD of the complete sketches became retail website Amazon's fastest selling pre-order DVD in its history.

Two of the sketches featured Lauren, one in which she toyed with *Doctor Who* actor David Tennant, the second in which she went to Number Ten Downing Street for work experience. In the others, lovelorn Elaine Figgis hooked up with *James Bond* actor Daniel Craig, Geordie Georgie tangled with comedian and Dawn French's husband Lenny Henry and won, while Nan appeared as a contestant on Channel 4's hit daytime game show *Deal Or No Deal*.

The most talked about sketch, of course, was the one where she appeared with then Prime Minister, the Right Honourable Tony Blair. However, the others were equally memorable and didn't have the whiff of being thrown together. If anything, they seemed to feature her characters at their best and funniest. The perfectionist in Catherine Tate had struck again. There was obviously no way she was going to parade her creations in front of a wider audience and find them wanting.

For sheer hilarity and brilliance, the *Bond Boy* sketch was right up there with the very best. The combined pulling power of Tate and *Comic Relief* was strong enough to secure the services of the publicity shy actor Daniel Craig, enjoying international fame as the world's most famous international spy. His pairing with the goofy-toothed loser in love who'd already married a Death Row cannibal and had been ripped off by an Egyptian chancer was inspired.

The set-up of the sketch is that she's met him through her favourite Eurovision chatroom on the internet. He was nuts about Celine Dion and, as Elaine believed she looked quite like her (post-surgery), she thought she'd give 'BondBoy68' a whirl. The idea that this well-regarded actor and suave incarnation of James Bond would be perusing Eurovision chatrooms and would be crazy about the Canadian diva and former Eurovision contestant is what makes this so funny. But, as she confides to the documentary crew: 'Well, he says he's an actor, but I've never heard of him. No, I think he works at Carphone Warehouse.'

Meanwhile, Craig sits on her couch, all doe-eyed and in love, occasionally getting up to make sandwiches with that well known brand of brown condiment Daddy's sauce and drink a Newcastle Brown Ale, and tells the crew: 'She doesn't know what I do, but she knows who I am.'

It's only after a camping holiday in Kirby Moorside, arrived at by tandem, that the cracks really begin to set in. He wants to stay in the tent and cuddle, she wants to see the sights. Back in her semi-detached in Leeds, it's not long before she's thrown the world-renowned heart-throb out on his ear, his teddy bear following a close second. 'Don't get me wrong,' she says, 'he's a lovely chap, but he's no John Nettles.' That she would prefer the ageing star of ITV's long-running cosy crime drama *Midsomer Murders* to James Bond seals the joke and says everything about Elaine Figgis' character. Seeing a movie star in such a drab setting, only to be rejected by Yorkshire's biggest spinster, was truly funny. Even someone who hadn't seen any of *The Catherine Tate Show* would have been able to appreciate this vignette as a self-contained story.

Fans of Channel 4's surprise ratings winner *Deal Or No Deal* would have lapped up Nan's appearance on the show. Hosted by former BBC golden boy, Noel Edmonds, it features twenty-two players who, every day before the show begins, each choose a numbered red box containing a different sum of money. One contestant is chosen each day, who then opens up the boxes in stages, being offered money from the never seen 'banker' after each round. Each box contains a different sum of money ranging from 1p to £250,000. The player must then decide to deal at the best moment in the game.

When Nan made her appearance, she was seen with a mixture of real contestants and actors. Things started off well, as they so often do with Nan, with her pronouncing: 'I'm on the telly, that's lovely innit.' She brought in a framed picture of grandson Jamie along with a piece of Madeira cake for Noel (Noel: 'I like the occasional nibble.' Nan: 'I've heard.') and a corned beef sandwich. However, she opted not to eat the latter in case of wind.

She then demanded a glass of Guinness and it wasn't long before she took a pop at the independent adjudicator, the woman responsible for sealing all the boxes and 'the only person who knows where all the money is.'

'Ugly cow, she is,' announces Nan. 'Sticking a bit of Sellotape on a box? Independent adjudicator? She didn't last long at school, did she?' She then proceeds to take out the 'Power Five' or top five sums of money in the first five boxes that made up her opening round, insulting every player who reveals the money.

Offered a very low £199, she shouts 'What a fucking liberty!' then immediately deals. When Noel expresses surprise at this early departure from the game, she reveals that she's already had a look in her box and there's only £50 in it. Refusing to play on, she then announces: 'Deal or no deal? What a load of old shit!' and staggers out of the studio.

For those who loved *Deal Or No Deal* this was a particularly good sketch. Tate's intimate knowledge of the show was obvious in the writing with Nan not only having a go at the independent adjudicator but also claiming there was no one on the other end of the phone when she talked to the banker. When asked in a *Guardian* questionnaire, 'When did you last cry and why?' she replied: 'I cry almost every time I watch *Deal Or No Deal*.' She has never made a secret of her love of all types of television, and it is this intimate knowledge and affection for the medium that often shines through in her work.

As well as Daniel Craig, there was another man who got more than he bargained for when he agreed to be involved in a Catherine Tate *Comic Relief* sketch. Lenny Henry, a familiar figure associated with the BBC's fundraising event since its inception, and married to Tate's *Wild West* co-star French, popped up in a Geordie Georgie skit. Who better to take on a high profile fundraiser than the patron saint of bonkers north-eastern causes herself?

In the sketch, Georgie waltzes in for her usual day at work, belting out *Something Inside So Strong*, Labi Siffre's song about Nelson Mandela – very appropriate for Red Nose Day. She then attempts to fleece co-worker Martin, her usual victim, for an all-night, al fresco sudoku challenge on behalf of the Barrow-In-Furness Medieval Jousting Association.

Why she's shifted her fundraising efforts to Cumbria isn't explained but it's all in a good cause, namely all the little African children who are addicted to internet gambling. Apparently, every thirty-eight minutes, one of them 'spunks his last bag of rice' on the 4.30 at Wincanton.

Martin is lukewarm in his promised donation when in strides Lenny Henry looking for cash for *Comic Relief*. Realizing that

Martin has handed him £150, Georgie takes his cheque, shreds it with Martin's own electric-powered paper shredder and head butts Lenny Henry with the parting shot: 'That'll give you a red nose!' Oh yes, Red Nose Day is a stressful day indeed for Newcastle's champion fundraiser.

Given her appearance in the previous *Doctor Who* Christmas Special, *The Runaway Bride*, it came as no surprise when the good Doctor himself popped up in the lithe form of Scottish actor, David Tennant, who had been playing the role of the Time Lord for the past year to great acclaim. Tennant and Tate had reportedly become good friends over the five weeks of filming and it would certainly be put to the test as he subjected himself to the full, sulky might of Lauren.

Striding into the classroom sporting a brown corduroy jacket and toting a very bookish-looking briefcase, Tennant introduces himself as Mr Logan, the new English teacher. Spotting his Scottish accent (Tennant is himself Scottish), Lauren wastes no time in going in for the kill, opining that she doesn't think he's qualified to teach them English, given that he's Scottish.

'Have we got double English or double Scottish?' As Lauren's questions go, it's quite a sensible one really. She then segues smoothly into: 'Are you the Doctor?' raising cheers from the crowd. When he comes back with 'Doctor who?' it's as rowdy as a Rolling Stones concert in the 1970s.

Lauren then accuses Tennant of being a 945-year-old Time Lord and asks him whether he's parked the TARDIS on a meter, and whether he fancies Billie Piper, his co-star in the TV series. Piper, one of the most popular Doctor's assistants, left to be replaced by Freema Agyeman. Writer Russell T. Davies also developed strong sexual chemistry between the Doctor and Piper's character Rose, a first for the science fiction show.

Not willing to take any of this lying down, Tennant calls Lauren pointless, repetitious and extremely dull, leading one to wonder whether Tate had taken some of the Lauren criticism on board and twisted it rather neatly for her own purposes.

What happens next demonstrates Tate's ability to take a simple formula and turn it on its head. Instead of her usual 'Am I bovvered?' routine, Lauren translates it into cod Shakespeare. 'Am-est I bovver-ed forsooth? Looketh at my face! Are you disrespecting the House of Cooper?'

She then recites a sonnet word for word and finishes with 'Bite me, alien boy!', thus bringing the house down. David Tennant, whom we now all know is the Doctor, then takes his only possible course of action, producing his sonic screwdriver and turning her into a tiny doll-like figure. Still, Lauren has to have the last word as the doll squeaks out: 'I still ain't bovvered!'

*

And so to that night's big-ticket item, Lauren's work experience with Tony Blair. Happening at a time when the prime minister's popularity wasn't exactly riding high after all the fall-out from Britain's involvement in the Iraq war, cynics suggested that this was a rather obvious move on his part to win back voters.

Writing in *The Guardian* a year after the event, Simon Hattenstone said: 'When Tony Blair was at his nadir last year, he knew he had to take drastic action to safeguard his legacy as the people's Prime Minister. So he did. He didn't withdraw troops from Iraq or lower taxes, he simply went on *Comic Relief* and did a sketch with Catherine Tate at Downing Street in which he said, "Am I bovvered?" It might not have saved him, but it was an inspired move. Blair was instantly transformed from the knackered old grump he had become to Laugh Out Loud Tony.'

As co-stars go, he certainly wasn't bad, not coming across as wooden at all and seeming rather to enjoy his little acting stint. As Tate joked afterwards: 'Tony Blair is one of the finest comic actors of his generation.'

The sketch begins with Lauren scuffing her feet down the pavement outside Number Ten, arriving rather later than expected for her work experience. When questioned about this, she launches into a long-winded explanation about Ryan's party being a 'mash-up', much to the woman at Number Ten's horror. Walking up the hallowed stairs, past all the portraits of former prime ministers, she asks, 'Who are these jokers?' and wonders if they're all Rory Bremner.

It's when she has to take tea and biscuits into the PM's office that the fun really starts. Interrupting his important call with three 'excuse me's', she then demands if he's seen anyone famous, before launching into a tirade about a shopping trip on Oxford Street and her own star-spotting. This includes references to Niketown, numpties and Center Parcs ('It's like Butlin's but you don't get wet.'). And then there it is: the prime minister of the country launching into his own 'Am I bovvered?' routine.

Wounded, but still desperate for Blair to ask her who's the most famous person she's seen, Lauren knocks over a bust on his desk and pronounces that it's 'rubbish here'. As she leaves, she can't resist popping her head round the door and finishing with 'It was Ross Kemp!' A former star of *EastEnders*, Kemp has gone on to win awards for his documentary series *Ross Kemp on Gangs*. The look of combined dismay, contempt and bafflement on Tony Blair's face says it all.

All in all, this was quite a coup for Tate. After all, you can't imagine Margaret Thatcher engaging in a skit with Ben Elton or even John Major sparring with much-loved veteran funny man Les Dawson. For a Prime Minister to have agreed to participate so fully in a sketch with a comedian was a first.

Speaking after the event on *BBC Breakfast News*, Tate recalled that the experience was 'surreal' and said of Number Ten: 'It was like a TARDIS...it goes back and back.' Given her in-depth knowledge of *Doctor Who*, she's definitely in a position to make the comparison.

There was no shaking in her boots beforehand though: 'I wasn't nervous because I don't particularly get nervous – I'm too busy thinking about what I've got to say – but there was a sense of occasion about it. We were all thinking: "This is history."'

The sketch even led to questions in the House of Commons. An MP asked Blair, in reference to some recent criticism of the then Chancellor, Gordon Brown: 'Isn't the prime minister bothered?' Blair's confident reply was: 'Fortunately, one of the things I haven't had to be bothered about in the last ten years is the running of the economy.'

Tate was later asked whether she thought Blair had 'used' Lauren for his own political purposes, but she didn't seem to want to be drawn on the issue saying, rather sarcastically: 'I don't want to sound naïve but do you not think he was just doing it for the little kids of Africa? Just give him the benefit of the doubt, eh? To have done a comedy sketch with the then serving prime minister of Great Britain was a brilliant thing to have done, for my memories.'

The fact that a picture of her and Tony Blair now hangs in her mother's flower shop in Bloomsbury proves how proud both she and her family are of the ground-breaking sketch. To be asked to be involved in not one but five sketches for *Comic Relief* must also have been quite a boost to the ego, not to mention how fast the resulting DVD sold.

As she said afterwards: 'It was quite a privilege, I was honoured.'

CHAPTER ELEVEN

Christmas Specials and Complaints

At 10.30pm on Christmas night 2007, some 6.4 million people sat down and prepared themselves to watch *The Catherine Tate Show Christmas Special*. These figures are quite astounding for a modern TV show. One of the highlights of the BBC's festive schedule, rumours had been circulating about its contents since the previous summer when it was filmed.

Most people knew that George Michael would be appearing as a special guest. And it had also been all over the tabloids that Lauren Cooper would be uttering her final 'bovvered' and breathing her last. Some papers had speculated that the pop singer would play a crucial role in her demise.

It's fair to say that the press, and the public, were as interested in Tate's *Christmas Special* as they would have been in a Morecambe and Wise extravaganza back in the 1970s or the latest seasonal episode of *Only Fools And Horses*. Tate was BBC's big gun as far as the seasonal schedule was concerned, and pre-publicity for the show had reached fever pitch. For the major broadcasters, the Christmas schedule is the biggest battleground. The networks go out of their way to try and ensure the highest viewing figures, and plan for many months ahead to put out the televisual equivalent of their finest silverware. That Tate was given a Christmas special was testament to how highly she was valued by the BBC. Only the best and brightest shows get their own Christmas specials, like the aforementioned *Morecambe and Wise* or the BBC's biggest banker for years, *Only Fools. Doctor Who* is another, of course, and is now one of the BBC's hottest properties, and Tate was to make her debut in that series in their Christmas special, *The Runaway Bride.* As far back as July, the *Daily Mirror* had run with the rumours of George Michael being Lauren's assassin, and it had even printed this touching obituary for the troubled teen (some of the details come from the imagination of the journalist rather than the backstory created by Tate): 'Lauren Jade Chardonnay Cooper was born in 1991 to single mum Faberge Cooper. The father is not recorded on the birth certificate, though a shortlist of possibles was drawn up. A precocious child, her first ASBO came at the age of six, along with a caution for shoplifting from Primark. A keen smoker and connoisseur of vodka-based fruit cocktails, Lauren's Facebook page listed her interests as "not being bovvered" and "disrespectin'". Briefly employed in a burger bar, there were hopes that she might actually make something of herself when she got to see the prime minister, Tony Blair, in 2007, but the meeting did not go well. Friends are asked to leave flowers from the 24-hour garage by some railings and also a teddy bear. If they can be bovvered.'

You know you've got a massive hit on your hands if a national newspaper is printing an obituary of one of your fictional characters some five months before her on-screen death is going to take place. So it's safe to say that expectations were running high for the special which could have been the last we'd see of these familiar characters on television. While Lauren was the only one to be officially killed off, with no plans for a fourth series or indeed another Christmas special, keen fans knew they might never hear Nan screeching 'What a fucking liberty' or Derek spitting out 'How very dare you!' again.

In the event, George Michael had nothing to do with Lauren's demise, although he might have ended up wishing he had. He turned up as a patient in Bernie's hospital and had to tell her to 'shut the fuck up' as she sang her way, badly, through Wham's hit *Jitterbug*. He then ends up doing a duet of The Pogues' *Fairytale Of New York* with her at the staff karaoke Christmas party before being forcibly made to smooch with her. Being forced to spend all your screen time in unflattering and ill-fitting stripy pyjamas and having to both sing with – and snog – Bernie the nympho nurse meant that he had to have a rather large sense of humour. As with other guests before, this would have done wonders for his image though. Most people had seen those paparazzi pictures of him lying on a steering wheel, pupils the size of saucers, after he was caught stoned at the wheel of a car in central London. A huge fuss was made of his drug-taking at the time so witnessing this animated and cheerful performance would certainly have helped to banish those less than flattering images.

In fact, his initial encounter with Bernie provided arguably the most laugh-out-loud exchange of the whole show. Clapping eyes on him for the first time, Bernie breathes throatily: 'Do you want my sex?' And he comes back, with an admirable sense of comic timing: 'Do you not read the papers, love?'

As for Lauren, instead of being seen off by the former Wham! star, she went to a watery grave after completely ignoring the advice of a local fisherman in Dorset. However, this was not before going into a lengthy routine about local yokels. Having announced 'I can well kayak!' as she, Liese and Ryan entered a river, she then started moaning about the countryside stinking of cows before spotting the fisherman. Asking him if he was a local yokel, she then went on to suggest that he was married to his sister and that his cousin was his mum. Ignoring his warnings that there was danger ahead, she plunged over a precipice, never to be seen again.

In the penultimate sketch of the special, we see grieving Liese and Ryan at Lauren's graveside as Bill Withers' *Ain't No Sunshine* plays evocatively in the background.

Other enjoyable moments included Geordie Georgie trying to raise money for doggers (people who enjoy watching others have sex in their cars or outdoors) by mounting a pedalo race from Whitley Bay to San Francisco – until she realizes that colleague Martin really *is* a dogger in his spare time, and Janice and Ray being forced to endure the indignities of eating *filet de salmon avec potatoes dauphinoise* for their Christmas lunch with Janice's sister Marilyn.

Special guests included Philip Glenister, detective Gene Hunt from *Life On Mars,* playing a policeman in Tate's spoof *Life At Ma's,* and Tamzin Outhwaite as a pal of 'absolute lunatic' Sam.

All of these passed off with nothing other than the chuckles they deserved.

However, there were two sketches that excited the wrath of some viewers, leading them to complain to the BBC and OFCOM (the Office of Communications – the independent regulator and competition authority for the communications industries in the United Kingdom). One of OFCOM's primary duties is to protect consumers from harmful or offensive material and it is where viewers can lodge complaints about what they see on TV – any series of reality show *Big Brother* usually has people calling in in their droves. The first complaint featured the all-cackling, all-swearing Nan Taylor, and the second the Northern Irish character John Leary's mum.

As each series, charity appearance and Christmas special passed, perfectionist Tate knew that she had to raise the bar. She'd heard some of the moaning about her over-reliance on catch-phrases and understandably wanted every show to be better than the last. Killing off Lauren was designed to end the relentless debate about the over-exposure of 'Am I bovvered?' And Tate had already expressed her fears about topping the recent *Comic Relief* sketch with Lauren doing work experience at Number Ten Downing Street. So Lauren had to go.

But what was to be done with Nan? She might still have been raising the biggest laughs with live studio audiences, but was there any way of making her even funnier?

The solution Tate came up with was to introduce Nan's daughter and Ryan's mum into the equation. The stroke of genius was to cast Kathy Burke, everyone's favourite London actress, in the role of daughter Diane. Having played everything from low comedy as Waynetta Slob with Harry Enfield to high art in hard-hitting movie *Nil By Mouth*, Burke is one of our most versatile and adored actresses. Her role as the hideously lovable Linda in sitcom *Gimme Gimme Gimme* opposite James Dreyfus also made her an obvious choice for the role of Nan's daughter Diane.

When she strode through the door of Nan's flat with almost identikit red hair and a cackle that matched Nan's in both pitch and ferocity, the live audience went wild. What followed was hilarious, if profane. After an apparently sincere ''Allo, Mum', ''Allo, sweetheart', the pair proceeded to rip verbal lumps out of each other behind each other's backs.

The long-suffering Ryan was joined by Diane's boyfriend Ranjit to witness the back-stabbing. Nan, in customary fashion, displayed appalling racism ('It's Indian. It's Indian fella. It's Indian fella in me front room. I've only got turkey. Is he allowed turkey? Is he allowed nibbles?'). She got away with this probably because we know the character so well and understand her foibles. As Tate once said of both Nan and Lauren: 'They would find fault with everything. It's that thing of privilege of old age and privilege of youth. You get to be belligerent and irreverent and everyone thinks that speaking your mind is par for the course.'

So while the rampant racism went largely unremarked, what did excite people's ire was the amount of swearing. As Nan and Diane got into a cursing duel, so the 'f' word count rose with Nan uttering it six times and Diane seven. This was rather a lot for one sketch but suited the characters and situation perfectly. That Nan's daughter was virtually a carbon copy, down to the cussing, quickness to take offence, mood swings, bad hair and back-stabbing, made this all the more hilarious.

The other sketch that prompted complaints involved the character John Leary's mum. She's the matriarch of a Belfast family whose son John has come out as a homosexual, much to her unexpected delight. Sketches detailing her over-enthusiastic response to his sexuality had run throughout the previous, third series.

The sketch that bothered people on Christmas Day was one in which the Leary family exchanged Christmas gifts. The granny was given a balaclava, the dad a knuckle duster 'for special occasions' and the mum herself an apron bearing the words 'Remember everything, forgive nothing.' Some viewers found this satirical exchange of paramilitary gear deeply offensive. Despite the long-running ceasefire in Northern Ireland, sensitivities still run high and this was a joke that some found not only unfunny but entirely inappropriate. John was given a replica of a man's genitalia ('It's a penis. But you can eat it.') while his granny, on discovering his sexual preferences, thrust some money into his hand with the immortal line: 'Get yourself a rent boy on me. It's Christmas.'

The fact that the show aired on Christmas Day, albeit well after the watershed of 9pm, was probably the reason some people took such offence. Forty-two complaints were lodged both about the swearing in the Nan sketch and the paramilitary-style Christmas presents. One complainer described the show as 'the most offensive programme ever broadcast on a Christmas Day' and one Conservative MP was moved both to write to OFCOM and to express her views to London's *Evening Standard*. As they reported: 'Nadine Dorries is very bovvered. The Tory MP for mid-Bedfordshire, who describes herself as the Tory answer to Bridget Jones, has begun 2008 with a bang. She has written to OFCOM to complain about the BBC1 *Catherine Tate Show* on Christmas Day. "After fifteen minutes of Catherine Tate, I switched off," she says. "It was offensive and violated the expression 'family viewing'. I thought of *The Office* Christmas special and how Ricky Gervais mixed pathos and wit with spectacular success. Catherine Tate didn't. On what is, whether you are religious or not, a day which is special to all, her own version of the Christmas special was astoundingly inappropriate. And so, I have begun the New Year complaining."'

It seems a bit unfair to hold a programme, broadcast an hour and a half after the watershed, up to the standards of 'family viewing'. But those complaining suggested that Christmas Day was an exceptional day on which many children were allowed to stay up late to watch television with their parents.

OFCOM launched an investigation into the complaints, eventually publishing their report in April, 2008. They concluded that the show had not breached broadcasting codes and that a voice-over warning of bad language before the show aired should have been enough to warn viewers. Part of the report read: 'Overall this episode was typical of *The Catherine Tate Show* and would not have gone beyond the expectations of its usual audience. For those not familiar with the show, the information given at the start was adequate.'

The John Leary's mum sketch was also given a clean bill of health in terms of complying with the broadcasting code. A statement was issued that said: 'In the case of the family from Northern Ireland we recognize that offence could be caused by focusing on any given community. However, in OFCOM's view it would have been clear to the audience that in a comedy show such as this, exchanging Christmas gifts of terrorist paraphernalia was absurd in the extreme. While it is appreciated that sensitivities still remain in Northern Ireland, comedy, especially satirical comedy, frequently explores the darker side of humanity. In our view this was the effect achieved by this sequence of sketches and consequently they were not in breach of the code.'

While she never commented publicly on the complaints or the investigation, Tate must have been relieved to be exonerated by OFCOM. The BBC had backed her throughout the controversy, and responded to the allegations of bigotry when it came to the Northern Irish family thus: 'Catherine Tate creates characters who are so over-the-top as to be almost cartoon-like and this is where her genius lies. Her comedy is never meant to offend any viewer and is always based on satire and grotesque exaggeration.' There may still have been a few Disgruntleds of Tunbridge Wells and Enrageds of Enniskillen unhappy at OFCOM's conclusions, but as far as the broadcasting regulators were concerned, Tate had done nothing wrong.

This wasn't the first time she'd excited complaints, however, and, with characters as outrageous as Nan and Lauren, it's hardly surprising. One outraged reader of the *Daily Express* sent this missive to his favourite newspaper, complaining of a BBC conspiracy to outrage public decency: 'Catherine Tate is full of swearing and *Never Mind The Buzzcocks* contains gay filth, while *Little Britain* features both of the above.' At least she'd avoided the 'gay filth' accusation...

The more serious complaints, though, inevitably revolved around Lauren, the popularity of her sullen catchphrase, and her impact on teenage behaviour. Tate admitted to the *Radio Times*: 'I get letters from teachers saying, "We really like your show, but please kill off that character because it's making our life hell." I also get letters from kids who say, "We love your 'Am I bovvered?' character, because every time our teacher asks us to do something, the classroom just shouts: 'Am I bovvered?'" Can you imagine? They write as if this is great!'

While Lauren was obviously a reflection of teenage behaviour that Tate had observed over the years, albeit a heavily exaggerated one, there were those who sought to blame her for creating the problem in the first place. Along with the nightmarish *Little Britain* creation Vicki Pollard, she of the shell suit and breathless 'Yeah, but no, but yeah' explanations, Lauren became a poster girl for all that was wrong with a generation of teenagers.

And it seemed that teachers were leading the accusations. In a 2007 poll for the Association of Teachers and Lecturers, staff believed that an increase in aggressive and confrontational behaviour among children was 'directly linked' to TV viewing. Catchphrases like 'Am I bovvered?' and 'Yeah, but no, but yeah' were being used by children to be rude and disrespectful.

It wasn't just comedies that were singled out, though. Claims were made that Channel 4 drama *Teachers*, a warts-and-all drama series that showed teachers and pupils behaving in an outrageous manner, had caused copycat bad behaviour. One teacher said: 'Their behaviour directly reflects what they see on television. For example, when on the *Teachers* programme a member of staff was slapped, we had two examples of this in our school the next week. We had never had this before in thirty years. Where else would this have come from? They acted as though it was acceptable.'

Whether there are direct links between TV programmes and bad behaviour is debatable, but disruptive behaviour was certainly a problem in schools. The same survey said that fifty-six per cent of staff had considered quitting because of disruptive behaviour, and fifty-four per cent knew of a colleague who had resigned because of it; more than one in three had been attacked by pupils, and one in ten had been injured and gone to the doctor; sixty-one per cent had been verbally abused or threatened, and twenty-six per cent had been subjected to 'intimidation'.

Given such a difficult situation, it's little wonder that the search for scapegoats was launched. But to blame Tate's mouthy yet deeply insecure character Lauren for turning an entire generation of teenagers into copycats is a bit rich. As Tate points out, Lauren never even swears: 'I don't think it's right. I realized kids were picking up on it and I feel bad enough that they're saying it ['Am I bovvered?'] in the classroom.'

Those letters from teachers must have struck a chord with her, though, given that she admits to feeling some guilt over annoying youngsters parroting her catchphrases. But she found a staunch ally in the form of *GMTV* presenter Lorraine Kelly, a woman known for her no-nonsense approach and vast reserves of common sense. Writing in her column in *The Sun*, Kelly said:

'Lack of parental control, drug addiction, poverty and poor education have nothing to do with young people behaving badly. No. It's all down to Catherine Tate's portrayal of Lauren 'Am I bovvered?' Cooper and *Little Britain*'s Vicki Pollard. If you believe the 'experts', these two made-up characters are responsible for the ills of modern society. I met a bemused Catherine Tate this week who has quite rightly chosen to treat this nonsense with the contempt it deserves. Catherine holds up a mirror to the world and her grotesque characters make us wince and laugh. To blame her in any way for kids behaving badly is downright bonkers.'

Tate was surely grateful for this heartfelt intervention of sound common sense. It must be hard at times to keep a grip on what is real and what is not when you're being praised to the rooftops on one side and pilloried for ruining society on the other. In her usual sensible manner, she has refrained from getting involved in any public debates or indeed slanging matches about whether her comic creations have had a negative impact on society. Given that similar debates have raged since rock 'n' roll first hit our turn tables, much to the horror of 1950s parents who thought it would end the world, it's probably just as well. Back when Tate was growing up, it was the then outrageous sitcom *The Young Ones* that was exciting social commentators to claim that Britain, and our manners, would never be the same again. This raucous comedy which saw a bunch of layabouts living a student-type existence of drinking, vomiting, blowing things up and generally being anarchic starred Rik Mayall, Adrian Edmondson and Nigel Planer – all of whom went on to have highly respectable careers.

These things have a tendency to blow over, just as glowering, hormonal teens have a tendency to turn into sweet responsible adults – most of the time at any rate. It's just a shame that we, and Lauren, will never get the chance to find out how nicely she might have matured.

CHAPTER TWELVE

The Big Screen

Having survived the wilderness years of bit parts and failed auditions intact, and gone on to conquer British television in some considerable style, Catherine Tate soon decided it was time for a new challenge. Even though she has described herself as a 'lazy control freak', she has clearly never been someone to rest on her laurels.

Many people, given the huge success and critical plaudits she garnered for *The Catherine Tate Show*, would have sat back and soaked up the attention and the royalties for as long as they thought they could get away with it. Never comfortable with fame, Catherine nonetheless knew that she didn't just want to be remembered for creating a gobby teenager and an equally mouthy old lady.

As a classically trained actress, her thoughts naturally turned to the next logical step in the career path: film roles. And with her heightened public profile and the general sense of being flavour of the month, it wasn't long before film-makers came calling. Given the closely guarded nature of such deals, we will probably never know what she turned down. It's likely that they included a host of projects that asked her to imitate, almost exactly, some of the characters she'd brought to the public attention. It is the patented wail of most actors that, once they become too closely identified with any one role, all people want them to do is something in the same vein. The career of many an ambitious ex-soap actor has foundered on these assumptions. Maybe it has to be somebody really special for a casting director to be able to see beyond the obvious commercial potential.

Suffice to say that Catherine, and her agent and advisors, were savvy enough not to fall into that trap. Given her television success and recognizability factor, there was something very valuable to market. And tied into her years of training and experience as a serious actress, this made a highly attractive package for any director or producer.

*

The first director to come calling was Alek Keshishian, the man behind the outrageous documentary *In Bed With Madonna*, the film that chronicled the antics on Madonna's 1990 Blonde Ambition world tour. He was casting for *Love And Other Disasters*, a London-set romantic comedy starring Hollywood star Brittany Murphy, an actress most famous for her role in teen comedy and box office gold *Clueless*. Murphy was to play Emily 'Jacks' Jackson, an American intern at British *Vogue*, who spends her life playing Cupid to all her friends while neglecting her own love life.

The role for which Catherine was approached was that of Tallulah Wentworth, an off-the-wall poet with serious emotional problems who would provide a lot of the comedy. After the first audition went well, she was called back for a reading with the Hollywood star.

As she recalls: 'After my screen test I was called back for what they called a chemistry meeting with Brittany Murphy. I wondered what I was going to do... get a Bunsen burner out? I thought it was wild but then I got the part. I walked on the set on the first day of filming wondering if it was for real.'

Also starring Welsh actor Matthew Rhys as Jacks's best gay pal Peter, the film was a kind of *Will And Grace* set in a glamorously shot London. That very popular American sitcom also featured a gay man and a straight woman locked into a very close relationship. Rhys, who is now famous Stateside for his powerful and funny portrayal of Kevin in smash-hit drama series *Brothers And Sisters*, adds a lot of dramatic weight to what is essentially a lightweight romcom. As its title suggests, *Brothers And Sisters* is about a close-knit yet often feuding family and also features former *Ally McBeal* star Calista Flockhart, veteran actress Sally Field and Australian superstar Rachel Griffiths.

Tate clearly enjoyed herself as the wayward and outrageous Tallulah, third wheel to the gay/ straight best pals, and she makes the most of the material. In one scene she gets to recite one of her excruciating poems to a packed gallery full of hideously embarrassed friends and strangers. With her black boyfriend looking on, she declaims: 'Meat. Big black dick in nice soft chick. I never knew the thrill I'd feel, knowing that I'd have to steal. You dangled your worm, I took the bait. This fish is caught, it's only fate. Die! Die! Die! White imperialist pigs. Aristocracy is pale and weak. You can't kill my love. He's black. He's meat.'

Anyone who can get away with that kind of material deserves a good reception and Brian Robinson, writing on the British Film Institute website, says: 'Catherine Tate gives a laugh-out-loud fabulous performance as a posh neurotic poet.'

Her *Wild West* co-star Dawn French also makes a cameo appearance in the film as a mad-as-a-bag-of-badgers therapist who bamboozles Peter by comparing the stages of relationships to farting. Other famous faces to pop up include former *Have I Got News For You* host Angus Deayton as the MC at a charity auction, Stephanie Beacham from *The Colbys*, *Lord Of The Rings* star Orlando Bloom and Gwyneth *Shakespeare In Love* Paltrow aka Mrs Chris Martin from Coldplay.

Tate and Murphy reportedly got on well on set which might have had something to do with the similarity of their backgrounds – albeit on different continents. Famous for her roles in hit movies such as *Clueless, Girl, Interrupted, 8 Mile* and *Sin City*, Murphy was born in Atlanta, Georgia, in 1977. Her parents divorced shortly after she was born and, like Tate, she too was brought up by a single mother, Sharon Murphy, and had little or no contact with her father. However Murphy started her career a lot earlier than Tate, with a singing role in long-running, globally successful Andrew Lloyd Webber musical *Les Misérables* at the age of nine, and she had her own manager by the time she was thirteen.

Murphy's early brush with showbiz obviously did not have a negative impact on her behaviour, however. Her impeccable Southern manners and warmth apparently proved a little too much for a typically hard-bitten British cast and crew. As Catherine said at the time of filming: 'She's genuinely, incredibly sincere but I think in this country we take that with a pinch of salt. She is genuinely adorable, but she will say to people who she doesn't know, "Have an amazing day." We say to her, "Seriously, people will think you are taking the mickey out of them if you say that with that level of sincerity because we don't really do that over here!"'

Love And Other Disasters was premiered at the Toronto International Film Festival on September 9, 2006. In 2007 it was released in France, South Korea, Poland, Israel, Spain, Russia and Bulgaria. But it was only on March 27, 2008, that it had its first UK screening at the London Lesbian and Gay Film Festival, undoubtedly due to the fact that one of its lead characters, played by Matthew Rhys, was gay. It looks unlikely to have a theatrical release in the UK, which is a shame as, while it may not be as brilliant as such classic romantic comedies as *When Harry Met Sally* or *Bringing Up Baby*, it certainly had its merits, one of which was Catherine Tate's performance as Tallulah. It does rate a 6.2 on the Internet Movie Database website though, which isn't bad for what is usually a very critical public audience.

*

Catherine's next three films were much more low-key British affairs and, like London buses, they all came along together. As she commented when all three were released within a week of each other in November 2006: 'It's a bit odd isn't it? Who knew? You can't have a grand plan about anything, and certainly films were never on my agenda. I was still reeling from the fact that the show had been successful, and here I am clogging up the nation's multiplexes. Everyone'll be going, "Oh, it's her again."'

It's a typically self-deprecating statement from Tate who a year earlier had exclaimed to an *Observer* journalist: 'I've done a romcom with Brittany Murphy! I mean, Brittany Murphy! Yeah!' It's far more likely that she knew that films were a good move career-wise but was far too modest or superstitious to admit this.

The next project she became attached to was *Starter For Ten*, a screenplay based on David Nicholls' best-selling, semi-autobiographical novel about a student who becomes obsessed with competing on *University Challenge*. The film was set in the 1980s, when the student TV quiz show was then presided over by the near-legendary Bamber Gascoigne and was shot at the Granada Studios in Manchester. Each week, two teams from opposing universities would face each other in a tough quiz that involved both academic and general knowledge questions. Much loved by the general public, the programme also gave rise to its own catchphrase 'Starter for ten', the number of points given to an opening question, and this became the film's title.

Although there are famously no guarantees in film-making, as the book had done so well it looked like *Starter For Ten* had more than a fighting chance at the box office. The fact that the screenplay was also being written by David Nicholls, who had worked on the cutting-edge thirtysomething ITV drama *Cold Feet,* further sealed its pedigree. Co-stars such as Charles Dance, famous from the movie *White Mischief* and a star of the BBC adaptation of *Bleak House* in which Tate had also appeared, and period drama veteran Lindsay Duncan, as well as cult actor from *The League of Gentlemen* Mark Gattiss playing Bamber Gascoigne, also helped.

Catherine was asked to play the mother of university student Brian Jackson, the lead role which was taken by heart-throb James McAvoy. She said afterwards: 'It was a bit of a shock at first to play his mum, as I'm only about ten years older than him.' A sterling job from the make-up department soon solved that problem though. She also says she owed getting the part to writer David Nicholls, of whom she is a massive fan.

Brian is a lad from Southend whose double-glazing salesman dad (James Gaddas) died at an early age and who has to work very hard to be clever and get a decent education. Tate plays Julie Jackson, his overly protective and doting mum who works in a shoe shop and won't let him leave for his first term at Bristol University without trying to press both bread and a chip pan on him. Her parting words: 'Try to eat a piece of fresh fruit every now and then.'

Brian goes on to experience all the pleasures and pain of University life, while gaining a place on the *University Challenge* team. When he returns home to the Essex coast for his Christmas holidays, he finds his mum happily soaking in a bubble bath with widowed ice cream man Des (the wonderful John Henshaw from BBC sitcom *Early Doors*). Tate lends a great deal of dignity to Julie, a woman with not much money and a lot of heartache behind her, trying to forge a new life as her son flees the nest.

She may embarrass him by turning up at the recording of the quiz show in Des's ice cream van, but when things go horribly wrong, she has his best interests at heart. As she tells him, without making it unbearably soppy: 'The people who really care about you don't mind if you make mistakes. It's what you do next that matters.'

It's a nice, low-key role that allows Tate to showcase her acting talents and should serve to make fans of her sketch show forget about her outrageous alter egos for a while. That was probably the plan.

When *Starter For Ten* was released on November 10, 2006, it got great reviews and did well at the box office. The *Daily Mail* proclaimed: 'To say that *Starter For Ten* is the best British romantic comedy of the year – which it is – is to damn it with needlessly faint praise.' The *Mail*'s film reviewer, Chris Tookey, also referred to Tate as 'the suddenly ubiquitous Catherine Tate', an epithet she'd surely predicted when she'd joked about clogging up the nation's multiplexes.

The reason for this reference to sudden ubiquity was the fact that not one but two films in which she'd appeared had been released just the previous week. On November 3, 2007 both *Sixty Six* and *Scenes Of A Sexual Nature* got their UK theatrical release. One was a bittersweet comedy about a boy's bar mitzvah in 1966, the other a romantic meander around Hampstead Heath looking at the lives of seven different couples.

The smaller role was in *Sixty Six*, based on a true story from the childhood of director Paul Weiland. Having made his career directing adverts, Weiland then branched out into comedy with some episodes of *Mr Bean* and *City Slickers II: The Legend Of Curly's Gold* as well as *Blackadder: Back And Forth*. *Sixty Six* tells the story of young Bernie Reubens (Gregg Sulkin), a younger brother who is obsessed with having the best bar mitzvah that London has ever seen. Unfortunately, it looks as though his plans will all come to nothing as the date set for his big day clashes with the World Cup Final in 1966. Could he be the only boy in the country not rooting for Alf Ramsey's boys to take the title?

As people still talk about what they were doing on that day some forty-odd years later, it's impossible to underestimate the significance of England winning the World Cup. It was a time of mass hysteria and rejoicing, and the players, like Bobby Moore, Nobby Stiles and Gordon Banks, became national legends.

It's a sweet comedy that stars Eddie Marsan (later seen in Mike Leigh's uncharacteristically upbeat *Happy Go Lucky*) as Bernie's tormented dad Manny, who is about to lose his family grocery business due to the arrival of big supermarket Fine Fare. As Marsan says of the script: 'It's an honest and beautiful tale. When I first met Paul [Weiland] and learned it was his story, I realized why there were so many layers to it. It struck me as such a universal story with so much to say about families and growing up.'

Helena Bonham-Carter plays his long-suffering mum Esther, while Tate is his cheery Aunt Lila. She's married to Manny's better looking and far more charismatic younger brother, Jimmy (Peter Serafinowicz – who now has his own eponymous comedy series on BBC2).

While Tate doesn't have a lot to do as Aunt Lila, a housewife who is as in love with her husband as the rest of the world, she again plays against comic stereotype. Her big scene comes when she offers up her much-vaunted catering for the bar mitzvah and it proves to be both unidentifiable as food and completely inedible. A born optimist, Lila takes this all in her stride and refuses to be beaten by her patent lack of success. She also looks totally at home in some beautiful 1960s costumes, her face and figure really being more suited to period dress than modern day garb.

While *Sixty Six* didn't set the box office on fire, it didn't receive a critical panning either, and Tate later said she had 'a blast' doing it. It was also the first time she had been in a script by writers Bridget O'Connor and Peter Straughan, who went on to craft her first lead role in a movie, *Mrs Ratcliffe's Revolution*, more of which later.

*

While *Sixty Six* was a low-key, period, feel-good family drama, *Scenes Of A Sexual Nature* was a bang-up-to-date screenplay with a sterling cast. Set during the course of a beautifully sunny day on London's Hampstead Heath, the camera follows seven very disparate couples as they play out their relationships as they stand at that time.

The cast reads like a *Who's Who* of British cinema, theatre and television: Ewan McGregor who'd made it onto the Hollywood A list in the *Star Wars* movies, Gina *Our Friends In The North* McKee, Hugh Bonneville who'd appeared in *Notting Hill*, Eileen Atkins, stage and screen star and co-creator of classic '70s series *Upstairs Downstairs*, TV veteran Douglas Hodge, *This Life* star Andrew Lincoln, Holly *Waking The Dead* Aird, Sophie Okonedo who was Oscar nominated for her role in *Hotel Rwanda*, Tom Hardy from *Black Hawk Down*, Mark Strong who'd also impressed in *Our Friends In The North* and Benjamin Whitrow, whose career stretched from *The Sweeney* to *Trial And Retribution*, were all happy to feature in what was a very low-budget production. Catherine plays Sara, whom we first see sauntering up to a park bench. The man she is meeting is trying to relieve himself in the bushes and has been approached mistakenly by a cruising man who thinks he is up for sex. Hampstead Heath is a notorious cruising area for men looking for gay sex – even George Michael has admitted to using it from time to time. Sara finds this amusing and we gradually learn that Peter (Adrian Lester) is about to be her ex-husband. Their daughter Eve arrives to join them.

The twist is that this is a couple who still like and fancy each other very much indeed, and it's a shock when they produce their final divorce papers. Peter tells Sara that she's always been the greatest kisser, and she is obviously very fond of him. It's only as they take their daughter for a walk on the Heath, dissecting their relationship along the way that we realize why they can't be together.

The other scenes include Andrew Lincoln and Holly Aird as a married couple who fall out as he eyes up a seductive French girl; Eileen Atkins and Benjamin Whitrow as childhood sweethearts who meet up by chance; Ewan McGregor and Douglas Hodge as a mismatched gay couple who discuss having children; and Hugh Bonneville and Gina McKee on a beautifully observed and awkward blind date.

The script was written by Aschlin Ditta, who had also worked on Channel 4's out there hospital drama *No Angels* and Tate's co-writer on her sketch show, which explains Tate's involvement: 'There's a huge personal connection for me on this movie. Aschlin Ditta wrote such a great script that everyone did it for no money.'

Her co-star Adrian Lester, who starred with John Travolta in

Hollywood presidential blockbuster *Primary Colors*, and who played Mickey in slick BBC drama *Hustle*, agreed about the quality of the script: 'It's clever, clever writing. I think he did a really good job on the script which means that, as you read it, you're looking at people that you feel you know, you're reading about people that you feel you understand and you're reading it and thinking: "Oh my God, don't do that!" You're also laughing at certain scenes that are hilarious.'

Given their easy chemistry in the film, it's amazing to learn that Tate and Lester only met on the day of filming. As Tate explained: 'Adrian and I met on the day filming started, and then just went for it. We wanted to catch, if we could, a nice, truthful and honest moment that takes place in human relationships. Hopefully, when audiences watch it they'll go, "That's me", or, "I know that guy", or, "I've been there."' She then goes on to joke about how she and Lester really got on: 'Actually, we kind of dislike each other really! We were just a bit lucky that we managed somehow to pull it out of the bag. God forbid they'd have caught our real chemistry!'

There's no rumour of any chemistry between her and co-star, Hollywood golden boy Ewan McGregor, either, but only because they didn't actually meet during filming. 'I didn't do any scenes with him, as he's not in my couple, but I met him at the press junket,' she explained. 'He was lovely – not starry at all. I think you're always disappointed when massive film stars are utterly normal. But he was lovely and normal and sweet.'

She's also keen to explode the myth that actors who work on films are necessarily worse behaved than those on television: 'The process is different but the people are the same. Often it's the same people you're working with in a film as it is on television – apart from Ewan McGregor, who's unlikely to pop up as a guest spot on *Casualty*. But actors are actors really. The luvvie tag is down to individuals. I do know people who are quite "theatrical". But most actors are grounded, sensible people who just occasionally have their stardust-and-glitter moments.'

Filming, as seems to have been the case on all her movies, was relatively stress-free: 'I think we got away pretty lightly really. We had the weather on our side and passers-by were really compliant to being asked to wait while we filmed something. Dogs didn't bark too much!' Once again, this was good preparation for her next project in which, this time, she took the starring role.

*

It was producer Leslee Udwin, who has the award-winning Britcom *East Is East* on her CV, who was responsible for casting Tate in her first leading cinematic role. After seeing Tate on the West End stage in Neil LaBute's *Some Girl(s)*, Udwin was certain that Tate was right for the part of the eponymous Everywoman in *Mrs Ratcliffe's Revolution*.

'It wasn't a play I cared for,' Udwin has said with admirable honesty about *Some Girl(s)*, 'but within that play Catherine was so good. She made me weep, she was brilliant, and she engaged me even if the play didn't. I knew she was the perfect Mrs Ratcliffe.' Tate played an ex-girlfriend of Schwimmer's character who imagined that he was still in love with her, leading to much heartache.

The role of Dorothy Ratcliffe is that of a downtrodden house-wife from Bingley, West Yorkshire, whose life is dramatically changed when her husband drags his entire family behind the Iron Curtain in 1968. The film was based on the true story of Brian Norris, who packed his family into a Russian Moscovotch car and took them to the then East Germany at the height of the Cold War, and Norris's daughter, Maggie, was a consultant and executive producer on the film.

Udwin had to fight hard to cast Tate, as she was then a relative unknown: 'Of course, there were all the pressures to cast an actress who'd won Oscars, which could only be Julie Walters or Brenda Blethyn or an American name. I just withstood that for all my worth. How could you cast an invisible English housewife, which is the essence of Dorothy, with someone who is so recognizable?'

It's astonishing to think that Catherine Tate was herself not a well-known figure at the time of casting. But at the time, Udwin saw in her a relatively blank canvas that could be filled in to create Dorothy Ratcliffe, a woman who undergoes a radical transforma-tion from unhappy, mousy housewife to take-charge heroine.

And she's back in those 1960s frocks with optional apron to create the authentic look. This is certainly not a glamorous role, but Tate is someone unlikely ever to have her head turned by superficial concerns. She leapt at the chance to clamber back into dowdy '60s gear, and all for the sake of the writing.

'The only thing you can ever do as an actor is look for the script,' she said. 'If it's a great story, which *Mrs Ratcliffe's Revolution* is, and if it's fantastically written, which this script is, then it's irresistible. It's the only real criteria about my work.'

The script was written by Bridget O'Connor and Peter Straughan, who had written *Sixty Six* and Tate was eager to have another chance to bring their lines to life.

Her character Dorothy is still deeply in love with her radical husband Frank, but it's obvious that his ardour has dimmed. She is also very out of touch with both her daughters, Alex (Brittany Ashworth) and Mary (Jessica Barden). Alex is a Lolita-type teen-aged temptress who is only interested in boys, art and dancing, while Mary is very much her father's daughter, hanging off his every word and just as in love with the idea of Communism as he is. Neither of them have much of a relationship with their mother, who spends her time cooking, cleaning, looking for some affection from her husband, and hoping for the best.

That is, until he comes home from work one day and announces that he's been offered a job in the DDR, or German Democratic Republic. The DDR, along with Hungary, Bulgaria, Czechoslovakia, Poland, Romania and Albania, lay behind the Iron Curtain. Allied with the Soviet Union, these were Communist countries that had no truck with the democratic West. After a brief family argument, the family, along with dysfunctional uncle Philip (Nigel Betts), set off in their Russian car to start their new lives under Communist rule. The guffaws of the border guards at Checkpoint Charlie as Frank explains what they're doing sums up the ridiculousness of the endeavour.

Frank is played by Scottish actor Iain Glen and he turns what could have been an unfeeling man into someone with whom you sympathize. A noted Shakespearean stage actor, Glen was attracted to the role partly because he wanted to do more comedy and he was a big fan of Tate as his co-star: 'She comes from a theatrical background and trained as an actor. Her comedy routine in the TV show became unbelievably popular and people just associate her with that. It is wise of her to move into film. She's fantastic in the role.'

It is his character's idealism that drives the plot but, as the family move into their hideous apartment in a small East German town, surrounded by huge rats and suspicious neighbours, the dream begins to fall apart. And when Frank is constantly told what to say in his job as teacher of English literature at the local college, the scales begin to fall from his eyes. As they watch the Stasi, the official secret police of East Germany, drag away perfectly innocent neighbours and as their own family falls under suspicion of not conforming to the totalitarian regime, things begin to reach crisis point and they plot their escape. The Stasi were much feared and used torture and intimidation to keep people in line. Many East Germans collaborated with the Stasi and the release of files in 1992 led many citizens to realize that their spouses, nearest and dearest, and neighbours had filed secret reports on them.

Locations were scouted in Germany for the filming of the movie, but it was decided that Hungary presented the best opportunities for recreating the former East Germany. Tate, who had never visited Hungary before, was surprised and delighted at the location. 'I must admit I was very surprised how cosmopolitan and Westernized Hungary was. It's such a beautiful country and the people were so interested in what we were doing – though of course they'd been living very recently with that censorship and intense rule. It was a joy to be there because of the architecture. There are so many museums and such a lot of culture to take in.'

She had got herself into a panic beforehand about what sort of food would be on offer, though, perhaps imagining that Hungary really would be like the script they were about to film. 'I went thinking there wouldn't be anything I could eat because I'm a vegetarian. I took a suitcase full of nuts, dried fruit, packets of Ryvita and peanut butter as if I was going to Siberia in 1942. But the first thing I saw at Budapest airport was someone eating a Magnum. It was very sophisticated.'

She had had some personal experience of life behind the Iron Curtain back in 1991, while on a student exchange in Russia, a time of great political unrest. 'I was in Russia, in Red Square, when the military coup happened. That was the closest I got to the kind of conditions we're talking about at that time. That was in the 1990s and it wasn't as bad. But it was a strange sensation because I was living with a family, and the father and his son went out to protest on the barricades, and for forty-eight hours we didn't hear from them. So, personally, in my domestic situation it was very frightening to see a family traumatized over where their menfolk were.

'The other strange thing was that however frightening, I knew that, as a British citizen, I was going to be protected from danger. As Westerners, we were marshalled into places where the military weren't and treated very well, so I was never in danger personally, but having built up this relationship with this family who'd taken care of me and to have such empathy with them, that was a strange thing.'

This unusual experience certainly stood her in good stead for playing a woman faced with the bleak conditions of the Cold War Eastern Bloc. From the timid yet stoic Yorkshire housewife, to the terrified woman facing all the challenges the DDR could throw at her, Tate is always convincing. But it's not just social and economic deprivations that she faces, but also the threat of losing her husband to a Communist floozy.

Tate plays the emotions of a wronged woman extremely well, with most of the pain and anguish communicated through those expressive blue eyes. But it is her transformation to a resolute woman who saves her family from ruin that makes the picture. The plot may be a little on the daft side, involving as it does comedy car chases fleeing from the secret police, and an unlikely escape via hot air balloon, but her emotional transformation is very real and convincing.

Tate had a lot of empathy for Dorothy and admired her spirit, however deeply buried at times. 'She's resolutely cheerful, and I suppose she's the kind of woman who gets sidelined a bit. As I imagine quite a lot of people in the 1960s in Bingley did – or anywhere. I think it was a fairly patriarchal society anyway. She is a housewife who ends up as a sort of mini revolutionary or dissident really, as she springs her family from East Germany. I don't need much more heroic than that, to be honest.'

That she met with Brian Norris and his daughter Maggie Norris, who had herself gone through the experience, obviously helped a great deal with the portrayal. The character of Mary, the youngest daughter who looks all set to become a Communist spy, is based on Maggie and it is this character that narrates the film.

As executive producer and script consultant, Maggie Norris was heavily involved in the production and Tate has said how important it was for her to meet and talk to her. And in a neat touch, Brian Norris played an extra in one of the pivotal scenes as an elderly Communist Party member at a town rally.

Maggie Norris is now a director herself and her credits include *Bad Girls; The Musical* based on the television series of the same name that premiered at the West Yorkshire Playhouse in Leeds.

As a mistress of different dialects in her sketch show, from Geordie Georgie to the Liverpudlian Ginger Woman, Tate should have found a Bingley dialect relatively easy. But, with actors from different backgrounds and areas, it was decided to go with a more general Yorkshire accent. 'There are Yorkshire dialects which are very, very specific and very, very broad, but if you put it on screen sometimes it sounds like a caricature,' she explained. 'So you just try and get the essence of where they are from, rather than getting it specifically from Bingley.' Let's hope that the good residents of Bingley weren't too insulted.

Some of the earlier scenes were shot in Halifax and Tate found this particular corner of West Yorkshire to be very welcoming indeed: 'I remember my mum came up and she still has a newspaper billboard which said, "TV Comic In Our Street." I hope that's the only time I'm on a billboard, given that they're not usually good news.'

Billie Eltringham, the director of the film also had a major panic when Tate's presence started to attract hoards of schoolchildren to the vicinity of filming. After all, who could resist seeing the woman who had created teenage heroine Lauren in the flesh? Said Eltringham: 'I was really worried because I thought they would all start squealing and actually, because she would always go and say hello, they were incredibly respectful.' Respectful! Gum-chewing Lauren would surely have been horrified at this outburst of courtesy and good manners. It's hard to imagine her, Liese or Ryan keeping quiet while a bunch of luvvies went about their business.

Tate was saved from homesickness during her location filming in Hungary as her partner Twig Clarke and Erin, then four, came to visit. Given her back-to-back filming commitments, this was probably a highly necessary trip.

Yet again, the filming of *Mrs Ratcliffe's Revolution* seems to have been a very positive experience for her: 'To be honest, we had such a laugh making this film, and the family unit we created was so real and so close, that it was a very "up" time. And we weren't away too long. It wasn't Communist boot camp!'

*

One of the reasons Tate may have enjoyed the experience of shooting these five very different films is the opportunity it gave her to relax and relinquish control. Acting is obviously a skill and an art form in itself, but to be able simply to act without the pressure of being responsible for the scripts and the end product must have seemed like a luxury.

Let's not forget that Tate moved from stand-up to co-star in a sitcom to being entirely creatively responsible for her own, eponymous, six-part show on national television in a very short space of time indeed. The pressure must have been immense. As someone who admits to being a great worrier, it must have been a hugely stressful experience. Even a bumptious, horribly well-adjusted egotist would surely have had problems with the time scale alone.

She admitted as much at the time, telling the *Daily Express* after *Mrs Ratcliffe's Revolution*: 'To be honest, it's been a complete relief to be given things that I haven't got to write, change or have an opinion on all the time. Instead of all that responsibility, I can just give my all to the characters, one character at a time.'

And however proud she is of her sketch show and the creations that burned their way into a nation's consciousness, she's canny enough to realize that she can't afford to stay still. As she approached forty, the irony of being most famous for playing a fifteen-year-old chav would not have been lost on her.

'I knew I had to mix things up and not be stuck with one kind of comedy. The show went so wildly beyond my expectations – but I still want to be able to do other things without people wondering if I'm going to say, "Am I bovvered?" whenever I make an appearance. You have to know when to move on...'

While none of these five films made a particularly big impact either at the box office or critically, neither did they do Tate's career any harm. By bringing her to a different audience, and proving that she could do serious acting as well as comedy turns, they should have helped her achieve what she wanted most – future opportunities to broaden her range. Even a pigeon hole lined with £50 notes is still a pigeon hole after all.

And even when the films were badly received, as was generally the case with *Mrs Ratcliffe's Revolution* – often panned for being too parochial and compared unfavourably with a film with a similar theme, *Goodbye Lenin* – Tate's notices were better.

As the critic from *The Guardian* noted in an otherwise sniffy review: '...this is rendered just about watchable by the talented cast: particularly Catherine Tate, who does a good job at humanising the put-upon housewife of the title.' This was an opinion pretty much echoed by the London *Evening Standard*, whose critic noted: 'Tate is best as a woman who finally finds her voice and turns her husband away from his mistaken idealism.'

So are we likely to lose this particular great British comic talent to the lures of Hollywood? Tate clearly likes making movies and it would seem to be the obvious next step, were the offers to be made. The jury is still out by the sounds of things.

'I would love to work there for the experience,' she said. 'The same as I'd like to work in Australia or France. But I can't see myself living there. There would be enormous pressure and it is not what I became an actor for. I've got a young family here, so I'm not really in the market for the LA scene. But it's a place I'd love to go and see if I was asked to do something over there. But I'm not about to go knocking on doors.'

With so many other British shows being transformed or potentially transformed into American versions though, it seems that it might be a possibility. After all, Matt Lucas and David Walliams of *Little Britain* fame have spent much of 2008 lounging by an LA pool having their talent courted by American producers.

Could we really see beloved Nan cursing in a Brooklyn accent though? Or Derek Faye mincing around San Francisco, repelling all boarders with an outraged: 'Gay, dear? Me, dear? No, dear!'

Come to think of it, the potential for the Americanization of Catherine seems pretty deep indeed.

CHAPTER THIRTEEN

Doctor Who

After first establishing herself as a national figure and talent to be reckoned with via her award-winning sketch show, it was difficult to see how Catherine Tate could improve upon this profile. Until, that is, we heard that she would appear in that treasured national institution *Doctor Who*.

Adored by fans worldwide, the science fiction show that had featured a succession of Doctors crime-fighting their way through space and time, had been around since 1963. Having run out of steam in the 1980s, it was successfully revived by writer Russell T. Davies and had become one of the most talked-about shows on television. To be associated with one of the BBC's hottest properties was guaranteed to boost anyone's career and profile.

Her initial engagement was just for the 2006 Christmas special, *The Runaway Bride*, but we already had a taster of her character in *Doomsday*, the last episode of the 2006 series. Her sudden arrival in the TARDIS in a wedding gown was a shock to everyone, not least the tenth Doctor played by David Tennant.

Given her comic credentials, Tate's casting at the time came in for some criticism as being for novelty value alone. Writer and executive producer Russell T. Davies was very determined to quash those rumours: 'One thing that people have been saying is that it's like a *Comic Relief* sketch, but it's not,' he told *The Guardian*. 'It's a proper hour-long drama and Catherine Tate has a proper part. She's amazing in it and she and David Tennant together are a joy.

As one observer has put it, a guest spot in today's *Doctor Who* is the equivalent of appearing on *Morecambe and Wise* in the 1970s. Any of the stars, such as newsreader Angela Rippon or classical conductor Andre Previn, who popped up on a *Morecambe And Wise* Christmas show was guaranteed plenty of headlines and a place in the nation's affections. In other words, it's a much-vaunted prospect and one not easily turned down. You can just imagine former *Morecambe and Wise* guest stars, Laurence Olivier, Glenda Jackson and Des O'Connor queuing up to take their chances with the Ood or the Adipose. In fact, maybe it's not too late… Watching the Ood's squid-like tentacles wrapped around Des's fake tan could be very entertaining indeed.

Tate certainly seemed to have no hesitation accepting, even despite the vagueness of the offer from the *Doctor Who* production team: 'I got the call and I said "absolutely" – not even knowing what it was, just that is was being something in *Doctor Who*. I didn't know it was a Christmas episode, I didn't know it was a bride, I didn't know anything about it, but I said "yes".'

As she admitted later, she's not even a lifelong *Doctor Who* fan, or Whovian as this very special breed is known. She later said on *Friday Night With Jonathan Ross* that she doesn't remember watching it as a child and was probably watching *The Basil Brush Show* instead. David Tennant, a self-confessed lifelong *Doctor Who* obsessive, quickly corrected her, telling her that Basil Brush was on *before Doctor Who*. You've got to love someone who knows that much about the show he's involved in and who isn't afraid to admit it.

What attracted her to the project was obviously the high profile of the series and the chance to work with two people she admired, writer Russell T. Davies and the latest Doctor, David Tennant. Prior to the screening of *The Runaway Bride*, she told *Heat* magazine: 'Well, I'm not an obsessive fan, but I used to watch it. For me, the big thing was to work with Russell T. Davies and David Tennant. The fact that it's *Doctor Who*, which is such an iconic thing, is brilliant.'

A former storyliner on *Coronation Street*, Davies had become one of television's most sought-after writers after creating the then shocking gay drama *Queer As Folk* for Channel 4 and romantic comedy *Bob And Rose* for ITV. A fan of *Doctor Who* since childhood, he had publicly stated that he longed to be involved in bringing the series back to life.

Davies is rightly credited with reinventing and rejuvenating the series in 2005 when it returned with Christopher Eccleston as the ninth Doctor and Billie Piper as his glamorous assistant, Rose. To cast such a hugely respected actor as Ecclestone and someone as famous and popular as former singer turned actress Piper, showed how seriously the BBC was taking this rebranding. After years in the doldrums with poor ratings and having been cancelled, they were preparing to come back with a highly publicized bang. This brand new, sharper incarnation of an old classic had sent the critics into raptures. Fans and critics alike were gutted when Eccleston announced he would do only one series, preferring to concentrate on other projects and worried about being typecast as the Time Lord.

Step forward David Tennant, best known for his performance opposite Sarah Parish and David Morrissey in the fresh and unusual BBC drama serial *Blackpool*. His obvious enthusiasm for the series and undoubted acting abilities made his transition into the tenth Doctor a lot easier than it could have been.

The chemistry between the Doctor and Rose (Billie Piper) was the stuff of newspaper headlines, office discussions and fevered blogging. Young, hip, feisty and blonde, Rose developed a crush on the Doctor and their unresolved sexual tension simmered throughout two whole series. But she, too, took the decision to leave, and it was in her final episode that Tate first popped up as Donna Noble.

In the Christmas special, *The Runaway Bride*, screened on Christmas Day 2006, we pick up the action where it left off in *Doomsday*, the last episode in the previous series. Donna is there in her wedding finery, having disappeared from her Christmas Eve nuptials to her boyfriend Lance (Don Gilet). She's surprised and extremely annoyed to be in a time-travelling telephone box with a total stranger and late for her own wedding. As the Doctor tries to get the TARDIS on track to get her back to her rightful place in the universe, all hell breaks loose.

Watching these events closely is the evil Empress of the

Racnoss (Sarah Parish, Tennant's co-star in *Blackpool*). A hideous, spider-like figure, she knows far more about what is going on than do the Doctor and Donna. What eventually becomes clear is that an unwitting Donna is the key to an ancient alien plan to destroy the Earth.

While the Doctor and Donna bicker throughout *The Runaway Bride*, they eventually come to an understanding, and the Christmas special ends with the Doctor asking Donna to join him on his adventures. She turns him down and we're led to believe that that is the end of the collaboration.

*

It was obvious from interviews she gave about the Christmas special that Tate enjoyed herself immensely aboard the TARDIS, however. While she joked that she was holding out for a summer season at the Wigan Rep but, as a summer job, 'this would do', the enthusiasm was bubbling not too far under the surface.

As she explained at the time: 'I'm Doctor Who's stop-gap assistant. In the last episode of the last series, Billie left and, at the last minute, this new girl arrives in a wedding dress on the TARDIS. We have these massive adventures and, at the end, the Doctor says, "Will you come with me?" and I say no. It was great just to do one episode.'

Filming in a heavy bridal gown throughout the unusually hot British summer of 2006 proved something of a trial however: 'I was hot in the wedding dress I had to wear but the supporting artists had to wear hats and scarves and gloves! It was so hot, it was almost illegal. I worried for their human rights!' She also said that running around in a bridal gown for five weeks was enough to put anyone off the idea of getting married.

Tate was excited to be interacting with the iconic *Doctor Who* paraphernalia though: 'To be inside the TARDIS was incredible – it was such a fun thing to do. I had a blast. She'd also never been involved in acting to invisible monsters either, but this didn't put her off. 'I'd never done blue screen or green screen, I'd never done that kind of acting. I'd never done a production where the special effects are so vast that they can't actually produce them until you finish the show. That was brilliant.' The unique challenges of filming with special effects are many. Instead of reacting to what the viewer sees on screen, some kind of scary monster, the actor must act to a blank canvas. Occasionally members of the film crew will waggle things on the end of sticks to represent the finished product, but this can be counterproductive and send the actors into fits of laughter rather than the appropriate terrified response.

While filming the special, which was largely done in the *Doctor Who* production base in Cardiff, heavy measures had to be taken to try and preserve secrecy. The BBC didn't want it getting out until they'd announced it officially that their comedy star Catherine Tate was about to join their iconic sci-fi show.

As co-star David Tennant explained: 'We filmed the first bit of her scene at the end of the last episode. Then, while everyone was at the wrap party, a handful of us crept back to the studio under cover of darkness. She was smuggled into Cardiff! Then, because of the schedule, we had to start filming the rest of the special before the final episode of the series was broadcast. We were filming on the roof of a building in London, high up, convinced someone was going to see us. Every secret was collapsing around us, but we managed to keep that one!'

This must have added an element of excitement to what was already a very high-octane production. Tennant was also very complimentary about his new co-star, saying at the time: 'I loved working with Catherine and I suppose that's what acting is about, you develop these new relationships. The show is different and just as good.'

She raved about him at the time too, and it could have looked like just another phoney luvvie love-in, until later events revealed that their affection and chemistry was real. The fact that he agreed to do a *Comic Relief* special sketch as Lauren's beleaguered English teacher also added authenticity to their claims of mutual admiration and respect.

She certainly didn't hold back when talking about the Christmas special: 'He's brilliant. He's fantastic. I love his work. I've watched him do so much stuff on stage, and I've probably followed his career more closely than he realizes! It was an absolute blast working with him.

Usually horribly self-critical and not keen on watching herself on television, she even admitted that she, along with the rest of the nation, would be watching the episode as it aired on Christmas Day. 'Oh God, yeah, I mean, I don't usually like watching myself on the screen, but this isn't about me. Whereas with my show, I'm really critical of stuff, this is just something I was part of and had a blast on. It's not a comfortable experience watching myself, but because it's *Doctor Who*, I'll do it.'

The Christmas special, and Tate's role in it, received a mixed critical reception and the 2007 series launched with a new, young assistant in the shape of actress Freema Agyeman as Martha Jones. Everyone at *Doctor Who* seemed excited at this new pairing and Russell T. Davies said at the time: 'The search for a new companion had been underway for some time when I first saw Freema Agyeman: she had come in to audition for the part of Adeola in series two. Watching her during filming confirmed what an exciting new talent she was, so under cover of darkness we called her back in to audition with David for the role of new companion. It was an immediate and sensational combination, and her range, presence and charm blew us all away. David and Freema are terrific together, and we're delighted to have chosen her to join the Doctor for more adventures in time and space.'

David Tennant seemed equally enthusiastic, saying: ' Freema was a joy to work with… She is not only very talented and very beautiful, she's great fun and I'm delighted she's coming on board the TARDIS full time. I can't wait to welcome her into the *Who* family.'

Playing Martha Jones, a medical student, who also had a fair amount of unresolved sexual tension with the Doctor, Agyeman lasted a whole series and was particularly popular with the younger audience. Then it was announced in July 2007 that Catherine Tate would be returning in the next series to play the Doctor's companion full time, although Agyeman would be returning for five episodes. This followed a rash of previous tabloid reports that Tate had never been asked if she wanted to do the role on a more permanent basis.

Looking back at how she reacted to press questions about why she wasn't becoming more involved, it seems obvious that she wanted to. 'They didn't ask me,' she told the *Mirror*, 'but I tend not to dwell on my failures. It was a fantastic job, one of the best things I've done, it was like making an action movie.'

In the same piece, David Tennant was said to be 'devastated' she wasn't offered the role long-term: 'They'd have made a great team, it's a bit of a shame. They don't get on very well at first but by the end they've fallen for each other.' Russell T. Davies merely said he knew that she'd be too busy which was why she wasn't asked: "She's got lots of other things going on. We knew she'd never have the time."'

All of these comments began to make more sense when on July 4, 2007 the BBC made their formal announcement. Under the headline 'Donna says, "I do!"', Davies confirmed: 'Catherine was an absolute star in *The Runaway Bride* and we are delighted that one of Britain's greatest talents has agreed to join us for the fourth series. Viewers can expect more ambitious storylines and a whole host of guest stars in 2008.' And Tate herself added: 'I am delighted to be returning to *Doctor Who*. I had a blast last Christmas and look forward to travelling again through time and space with that nice man from Gallifrey.'

Apparently, Davies had been flabbergasted that Tate would even consider joining the show full time and it was only after a phone call from the BBC's Head of Fiction that he realized it might be a possibility. 'We had no idea Catherine was going to come back to us. We couldn't believe we got her for the special really, she's so in demand. And not just that, Catherine generates her own stuff, she's a writer too, so she's always busy. It came about after Catherine had a meeting with Jane Tranter, BBC Head of Fiction. Jane rang me and said Catherine had gone on and on about *Doctor Who* and how much she'd enjoyed the special. Jane said, "If you ask her to do the series, I think she'll say yes."'

Davies was still unconvinced and thought Tranter had got the wrong end of the stick entirely: 'I thought it was ridiculous, but my colleague Julie jumped on a train to go and meet with Catherine. I didn't go because I was busy saying, "Don't be ridiculous, we'll never get her."'

But Catherine had agreed to a whole series and cancelled all her plans there and then.

*

And so Donna Noble sprang back to life and had to be given a more fleshed-out identity and a story arc that would carry her through an entire thirteen-part series. This was essentially Davies's job, and he jumped at the chance to do something a bit different with the Doctor's assistant.

As Rose and Martha had both been a little bit in love with the Doctor, he found it refreshing to be able to take away the sexual chemistry and take it in a different direction. 'There's a danger we could settle into a rut,' he said. 'That's why we've started each series with a new set of lead actors. It reinvigorates the show. I love the fact that Donna's a little bit older than the Doctor, and that she's not in love with him, as our other companions have been each to some extent. He needs a challenge.'

His excitement at writing for Tate seemed genuine too: 'She's absolutely fantastic. That's why we wanted to bring Donna back and why I wanted to write more for her. Obviously Catherine can do comedy with her eyes shut, but when she hits the tragedy – and there's a lot of tragedy for her character – Catherine gives the most stunning performance.' Mind you, Davies is clearly an excitable man and no stranger to hyperbole, as he's quick to rave about his star David Tennant too. 'There's a danger we don't talk about David often enough. He's so powerful and brave and scintillating as the Doctor, there's almost a danger of him blinding everything else.'

The idea of the Doctor having his first equal partner was one that interested Davies very much, and it was a much more modern way of approaching the series. 'It's about time we got someone in the TARDIS who is not so doe-eyed,' he has said. 'Donna is much more the Doctor's equal than any of the previous assistants. She is older and she is not in love with him, and that also makes a difference. David's Doctor is now so glittering and stellar that he needs bringing down to earth by someone who can question him. In episode two, Donna changes the future of characters by her strength of will. I don't think any other assistant could have pulled off that scene.'

Given the history of the Doctor's assistants – most have been young and glamorous, and all have kow-towed to his greater wisdom – Donna came as a bit of a shock to a seasoned *Doctor Who* audience. But Davies thought she would work and connect with an audience because she is more like them, and, in fact, represents the person on the sofa: 'She experiences real moments of terror. She is flawed. It really is like having me or you on the TARDIS.'

*

There was obviously a great air of excitement over proceedings as shooting commenced on the fourth series of the new *Doctor Who* in the late summer of 2007. While there might have been a lot of cynical adult carping about just what a woman of nearly forty, and a comedian to boot, could bring to the role of the Doctor's assistant, others were more impressed. She made a huge hit with some younger viewers in Cardiff when she popped round to an old lady's house for tea.

On one particularly cold day, grandmother Wendy Lewis in North Cardiff got a surprise knock on her door. Producers from *Doctor Who* had come calling to ask if Catherine Tate could take a forty-five-minute break from filming as she was freezing. Mrs Lewis was happy to oblige and had the presence of mind to get in touch with her grandson Ross Lewis at his nearby school. It's not recorded what the teachers thought of Ross and his two friends, Victoria Spernaes and Yasmin Akbari, cutting classes to rush to Wendy's house and meet the woman behind the 'Am I bovvered?' catchphrase. But the trio were delighted and couldn't have been more shocked if Catherine Tate had arrived at the end of their street in a TARDIS.

Ross, who is fifteen, said afterwards: 'She was so funny, absolutely wicked and really down to earth. She made herself comfortable and put her feet on the sofa. She didn't mind signing autographs or posing for photographs. Yasmin was so surprised she said, "Oh, my God!" and then Catherine repeated it straight away in the voice of Lauren. My friends couldn't believe it, they were just so shocked.'

He also had the presence of mind to ask her what it was like to interact with the Queen at the Royal Variety Performance: 'She told me she thought she was going to be locked in the Tower that night because she didn't know how the Queen would react. Catherine had tea and my nan's Welsh cakes, then she came back and asked for more to take away. It was as if I had met her a dozen times.'

She even made jokes at the director's expense for the children's amusement when he came in to discuss the next scene. 'Catherine wasn't looking at him but had a concentrating face on and was tucking into a Welsh cake. As soon as the director left the room she turned to the three of us and said, "I didn't get a word of that – did you?"'

This story amply demonstrates Tate's ability to connect with a young audience. This was obviously a vital part of her appeal as part of the *Doctor Who* package, and something that the powers that be couldn't have failed to realize. With her rebellious teen character Lauren now an established part of the national consciousness, she already had a head start in winning over the hearts and minds of the children who make up the bulk of the Saturday night sci-fi audience.

As well as scoffing Welsh cakes at every available opportunity, Tate also enjoyed playing cards between takes and clearly had a whale of a time hanging out with David Tennant and the rest of the cast and crew. She has said of him: 'You couldn't wish for a better colleague. When *Doctor Who* first returned a few years ago, Christopher Eccleston came in and was brilliant. But now David has done something extraordinary with it – he's taken it to another level.

It was a level she was happy to shoot for herself, whatever she may have thought of his competitive nature, as demonstrated in this description of between-takes relaxing: 'Between each take we all rush out to play cards. David is very competitive – we did contemplate playing for money, but people are so cut-throat it would get ugly.'

Clearly in a jovial mood about the *Doctor Who* experience, she also joked to *Elle* magazine that she hardly had to spend any time learning lines: 'There aren't that many to learn because my scenes in *Doctor Who* often just involve hanging from a wire or running away from an imaginary monster, so all I do is practise my face.' Anyone who has seen any of the fourth series and witnessed the huge part she plays in it will realize that she really was being ironic.

When questioned about why she chose to come back for a whole series, she was relaxed and sincere in her responses. And why not? A major role in an iconic television drama gave her the chance to prove herself as an actress to a much wider audience. 'It was a no-brainer,' she said. 'Working with David Tennant on Russell T. Davies's scripts is the best possible double whammy.' She says her invitation to return came as a surprise though: 'I wasn't expecting to be asked back, just because I didn't have any idea that the character would have another life beyond the Christmas special. It's pretty much a once-in-a-lifetime offer to go time-travelling and Donna just kind of thinks, "What have I done?" But everyone thinks "what if" about a lot of things in their lives. Donna's very lucky – she gets to live her "what if?"'

She really liked the character development for Donna too, another pat on the back for Russell T. Davies. 'Donna is feisty and independent-minded. She won't take any nonsense from anyone. Donna's funny, so I'm able to bring a lightness of touch to her. The idea of coming back and seeing what had happened to Donna since Christmas really appealed.'

Tate neatly sums up what an excellent career move *Doctor Who* was for her with this praise, again, for Russell's scripts: 'They're superb. In the 1980s *Doctor Who* felt tired and dated and it fizzled out. But Russell has managed to revive the show by completely shaking up the format. He writes such marvellously witty dialogue. It's a great mixture of drama and comedy, so it's giving me brilliant opportunities for straight acting. It's quite a nice bridge for me. I love comedy sketches and I don't want to distance myself from them, but this places me in an area where people aren't used to seeing me.'

She received criticism after the Christmas special for perhaps shouting her way through it, and one cheeky interviewer from *Heat* magazine asked her if that was going to continue: 'Not as much, because that story was self-contained. If you had thirteen episodes of someone just shouting, they wouldn't have much of a character arc! And Donna certainly does in this series. She goes on a great personal journey, which was wonderful to play.'

She was also relieved not to have to play out all the 'will they/ won't they' mushy stuff on screen: 'She doesn't view him through a romantic filter. They're mates. I think that was a very conscious decision by the *Who* team, because those stories have been played now.'

No matter how much Catherine Tate relished playing the role of Donna and becoming a more permanent part of the *Doctor Who* team, she cannot have been prepared for the avalanche of criticism and comment that came her way. After the Christmas special, when her longer-term casting was announced and when the series launched, everyone from grannies in Lanarkshire to sober-minded commentators for right-wing journal the *Spectator* to everyone with access to the internet had an opinion on whether she was up to the job. For someone as sensitive as Tate, this must have come as something of a shock. Although she was beginning to understand the significance of *Doctor Who*, and appreciate its many good qualities, she can't have realized how important it was to so many people.

Given the amount of hurtful stuff that was written and said, it is small wonder that she claims that she never reads her press, and that her friends and family know better than to mention anything they've seen or read. If you weren't on the receiving end of it, it would be almost funny, especially given how seriously the normally high-minded broadsheets seemed to take the issue. You can imagine her wanting to scream: 'It's only a drama for God's sake. It's only television! Nobody died!'

A writer in *The Spectator* summed up his feelings after watching the first episode thus: 'And now she's arrived just how bad and annoying is she? Well, the good news is: not as bad and annoying as you might have feared. But, given how bad and annoying you feared she would be, I'm not sure that's going to provide total consolation.' Talk about not giving someone a fair trial.

Unsurprisingly, the writer's major objections seemed to be that Doctor Who's assistant should assume a more traditional, feminine role and he complained at Davies's '...insistence that Doctor Who's female assistant should not just be there to scream, get captured and be rescued, but should be a rounded, valid person who in her intuitive, clever, feisty female way is every bit as important and interesting as the Doctor himself. But it's not called *Doctor Who And His Interesting, Feisty And Equally Valid Assistant*. It's called *Doctor Who*.'

The chorus of criticism was taken up by the mid-market and tabloid press too. David Stephenson, writing in the *Sunday Express,* opined: 'The scripts are great, production values are still high, David Tennant is brilliant but what on planet Earth is Catherine Tate doing there? You might as well cast Al Murray as Doctor Who (OK, I would watch that). Her character reminds me of one of those bolshie *Apprentice* candidates who hasn't yet discovered the world is round, or a crazy Whovian from a *Doctor Who* convention. This role needs an actress, not a comedian. We can only hope that this apparently ratings-proof series survives this gaffe.'

Over in the *News of the World*, TV critic Ian Hyland was no kinder: 'A trip back to Pompeii at *Doctor Who* where an overbearing force of nature with a flaming red top was about to erupt and ruin everything. But enough about Catherine Tate. OK, OK. So she was almost bearable this week... but to be fair, near the end I still thought she'd broken into full-on, foul-mouthed

Cockney Gran mode when she yelled, "Doctor, you can't!" after the Doc said he was going to let everyone die.'

Back in the broadsheets, A. A. Gill was funnier and more even-handed as he applauded the decision not to go for romance: 'Catherine Tate is the latest assistant. She looks and sounds far more extraterrestrial than he does. She's positively stratospheric, and her performance is like a chicken coop in a thunderstorm. I did like the ending, though. They played it awkwardly straight, because they didn't fancy each other and were only mates in the sharing-sherbet-dip-dabs sense. All over the country, I could sense the ten-year-olds' relief. Thank God, no kissing or sloppy stuff.'

On social networking site Facebook there was even a user group called 'I hate Catherine Tate and she shouldn't be in the new series of *Doctor Who*.' If Tate knew about this, how bizarre a prospect must that have been for a working actress? To be vilified merely for taking on a role?

Doctor Who forums on the internet positively crackled with outraged fans calling for her to be removed too, a fact picked up by *Daily Express* columnist Virginia Blackburn. Her opinions fairly burnt through the page: 'Glory be, *Doctor Who* has returned to our TV screens. But what's this? The ghastly Catherine Tate is at his side. What was the BBC thinking of, putting this charmless, grating lump in the best programme on the box?' She goes on to describe Tate as Donna as 'dreary and unlikeable' and urges Russell T. Davies to get rid of her, and fast.

Even London listings magazine *Time Out* waded into the debate, with one writer claiming that Tate was far too old for the role. Said Juliet Bowbrick: 'Catherine, how does it feel to know that you're going to turn off every young girl from seven to seventeen from watching *Doctor Who*? I don't want to say it, but I'm going to have to: Tate (as Donna) is too old to be the Doctor's sidekick. The only female role model in the show now looks like your mum, running around in ill-fitting clothes and shoes from M&S, chasing a bloke who'll never fancy her. I can hear the children in the playground shouting: "Who wants to play *Doctor Who*? Bagsy not be Donna."'

It can't only have been Catherine Tate who found this tide of often very personal criticism distasteful. A lot of viewers decided to give the new series, and Tate, a chance and viewing figures were excellent with the first episode of series four picking up 9.14 million viewers. As we got to see more of Donna in all her dimensions, so audiences and critics softened.

Some hardcore Whovians remained set in their ways and couldn't stomach a Doctor's assistant who didn't sigh at his feet. But others enjoyed the humour and warmth she brought to the role and came to appreciate that *Doctor Who,* like all things, must move on to survive.

Catherine Tate bowed out at the end of the fourth series. Having briefly been half Time Lord, half human, Donna returned to Earth with all her memories of time travelling wiped forever. As her character will die if she's ever reminded of these times, it seems unlikely that Donna, or Tate, will ever return to the TARDIS. There will be a Christmas special at the end of 2008 but no full series confirmed in 2009, merely a selection of specials. Russell T. Davies has said he will stand down, but feels there is twenty years of life left in the series if it's looked after sufficiently and revamped every now and then.

While Donna will not make it through the next two decades, let's end on a positive note. After seeing her in the first episode of the fourth series, one young viewer was sufficiently moved that he sent this letter to *The Sun* newspaper, winning him both a national forum and a £10 prize. 'I would like to pay tribute to the explosive beginning of the new series of *Doctor Who* on BBC1. David Tennant and Catherine Tate are outstanding, while Sarah Lancashire was a great guest-star as the sinister Miss Foster. Also, the animation of the fat-busting aliens – the Adipose – was excellent. I think Donna is a great companion for the lonely Doctor! Callum Brown (aged 10), Middlesbrough.'

Had this been brought to her attention, she would surely have been appreciative of such a loyal and enthusiastic fan and it may have helped her blot out the naysayers.

CHAPTER FOURTEEN

Famous Friends and Other Fans

In the spring of 2005, Catherine Tate was offered a theatre role she could only have dreamed of when she was playing yet another nameless whore at the National Theatre. She was asked to play one of David Schwimmer's ex-girlfriends in *Some Girl(s)*, a play by American dramatist Neil LaBute at the Gielgud Theatre in London's West End.

Schwimmer, of course, is globally famous for his long-running role as Ross in American sitcom *Friends*. As a long-standing fan of the show, Tate couldn't believe who her latest co-star was going to be. *Friends* was one of the longest-running and most popular sitcoms on American and international television, and made global superstars out of its ensemble cast of six. She documented her understandable excitement at this turn of events in a very funny and extremely effusive essay in the *New Statesman* in June of that year. What she couldn't have predicted was that some of her words were to be taken out of context and blown up into a non-existent 'feud' between her and her Hollywood colleague.

What Tate actually wrote ran as follows: 'When I found out I was going to be working with David Schwimmer – more commonly known as Ross from *Friends* – I could barely contain myself. I was the most excited I've ever been about any job...'

Clearly thrilled by what she considered to be a 'great part' in the new Neil LaBute play *Some Girl(s)*, Tate at first tried to play it cool when she first attended rehearsals, concerned that the rest of the cast would think her unprofessional if she showed how tremendously happy she was to be involved with the play and appearing with David Schwimmer, an actor for whom she held a great admiration. She claims to have been desperate to ask Schwimmer all about *Friends*, but because she was aware that his career had progressed and that he wanted to look to the future, Catherine resisted the temptation.

During their first rehearsal together, Catherine had to sit on Schwimmer's lap and recalled how she tried to take as much of her own weight on her own legs as possible, worried that Schwimmer might compare her to the famously slim Jennifer Aniston, who had played Rachel in *Friends*, the on-off love interest of Schwimmer's character, Ross, and who was at one time married to Hollywood superstar heartthrob Brad Pitt.

While it is unlikely that Schwimmer should want to weigh every actress with whom he works against Jennifer Aniston, Catherine held back not only from sitting fully on his lap but also from trying to strike up a proper friendship with him for fear that she might embarrass both him and herself by appearing to be more of a fan than a professional. 'Any conversation we have off-stage is of a very cursory nature,' she wrote, 'and all eye contact is kept well and truly to a minumum. And all because I was too embarrassed to let him know how great I think he is.'

What the papers picked up on was the line about Catherine not being able to make eye contact with Schwimmer. Ignoring the comedic context of her comments, they whipped up an imaginary feud between the new BBC star and the American household name. Headlines like 'Not Such Good Friends' and 'He's No Friend Of Mine: Co-Star Blasts Ross' appeared all over the press, leading people to believe that the pair were at loggerheads. Tate was horrified and understandably so. She had been honest about how star-struck she had felt and tried to make a joke out of it, only to be caught up in a maelstrom of fabricated nonsense.

She was then put on the spot and came out with this explanatory statement, lest the so-called 'feud' be blown up any further: 'Of course I like David, he's a very funny, personable man, and easy to get along with. I am a bit like a rabbit stuck in the headlights when I'm with him, but I don't think my article went too far, it's been misconstrued. It was meant to be a self-effacing account of how I've tried to be too cool in his company. If we'd really fallen out, I wouldn't put it into print.'

Having starred in America's biggest sitcom for twelve years, Schwimmer was used to such non-stories from the press and took the whole thing in his stride. He rang her up the day the story broke to reassure her that he knew it was all nonsense, which must have calmed her down somewhat. The whole incident did a lot of damage to her relationship with the press though, and she's been notably more guarded ever since, restricting her bigger interviews to the broadsheets rather than the tabloids. She told the *Radio Times* afterwards: 'What I said was, "I admire him so much I can't look at him" and it came out, "I just can't look at him." What the hell, it's chip paper.'

Just prior to this though, she really let her excitement bubble through at working with someone she'd admired in her own living room for so long. She told a magazine: 'If someone had said to me last year that I'd be working with Ross from *Friends*, I'd have thought that was a fantasy.' She went further with the *News Of The World*, joking: 'When *Friends* was on I was convinced we'd get married. Then I met my partner, Twig, had a baby and thought it would be tricky but that David probably had a good lawyer who could sort it out. Now I've met him, though, I don't fancy him – and I really wanted to! We have cast get-togethers but he doesn't come out much. I never mention *Friends* – it's like "Don't mention the war!" The way I deal with working with someone I'm a fan of is by ignoring them and reading the paper.' It's a shame that this experience taught her to be more guarded in interviews where her comments were often very funny, but could obviously be misconstrued. However bruising, it was probably a lesson well learnt.

Other than this incident, she enjoyed the thrill of being in the West End again in live theatre, confessing it was a relief to leave behind her own show to star in someone else's work. However it wasn't without reservations: 'It's like the grass is always greener for me. When I've had the responsibility of doing my show I often daydream about the joy of just being handed a script and asked to turn up for rehearsals. And then the weeks [of the play] go by and you forget about the stress and strains of doing that because you're in a position where, however open and helpful everyone is, it's not my show, it's not my gig.'

Having said that she was amazed to get the part, she was further flabbergasted when the playwright himself rang her up and asked for her input. Neil LaBute, an American film director, screenwriter and playwright, and the man behind *In The Company Of Men* and *Nurse Betty*, thought she might have some ideas. 'Neil LaBute rang me when I got the job and said, "I'm really pleased you're doing it, let me know what you think of the script, if you've got any ideas!" Like I'm going to! Like I'm going to ring him up and say, "Listen Neil, I think we need a couple more gags here – think you've missed a trick there, Neil boy!"'

Having seen her performance, LaBute was more than happy with it, going on record with this glowing reference: 'She's got that perfect blend of comedic and serious. And she's really adept at understanding that you need to leaven the heavy stuff with humour. Not just because it's a nice mix, but because it unbalances the audience, takes them on a different ride.' And her co-star, the man she'd once dreamed of marrying as she watched his on-off screen relationship with Jennifer Aniston, was equally generous with his praise. Schwimmer said at the time: 'Everyone knows Catherine as a great comedienne, but when they see her in this play they will be blown away by her performance. I've been a fan of hers for a while as I record her show at home and love her range of characters. My favourite is when she plays the old granny – she kills me.'

What a wonderful vignette that conjures up. Tate at home in her dressing gown and slippers, tucking into a tub of Häagen Dazs and fantasizing about marrying Schwimmer, while he reclines in his New York apartment laughing himself silly at the filthy mood swings of Nan. If you needed any proof that life was indeed strange, this would seem to be it.

Her generosity with friends was also demonstrated in the casting of *Some Girl(s)*. When one of her co-stars had to drop out, she suggested Sara Powell, an old drama school mate, to step in. Powell was very grateful for the recommendation, and equally as fazed by the *Friends* connection: 'Someone dropped out and they had to re-cast, so Catherine suggested me. She's great. She was funny as hell at drama school. David was fantastic to audition with – it was difficult to be intimidated because he was so into the role. He wasn't about being a star. It was only afterwards I came out and thought, "Oh my God, I've just auditioned with David Schwimmer!" This starstruck business is obviously catching and not just restricted to members of the public...

The other women in the production were Lesley Manville, who had worked with revered British director Mike Leigh, and Saffron Burrows, now a regular on hit American law series *Boston Legal,* and neither managed to get into a fictional feud with the great man. With her usual self-deprecation though, Tate admitted to feeling inadequate around the younger, slimmer Burrows, particularly when it came to a photo-shoot, something she's on record as loathing.

'I instinctively feel cautious about a request that comes in for myself and Saffron Burrows to do a photo shoot for a fashion magazine. I say no. The thought of posing for pictures clad in the latest trends fills me with panic. I'm not entirely sure what a fashionista is, but I'm fairly sure I'm not one. It's not that I'm not flattered to be asked, it's just that I'd rather scrub floors than do it. And I hate scrubbing floors. Our company manager dismisses my refusal and assures me it will be fun. The dreaded morning arrives, my heart starts racing and I feel sick. I look at the rails of designer evening gowns and decide that nothing is going to fit me. Everyone rides my tetchy negativity with good humour and grace. But I feel dreadfully awkward. It's one thing being photographed wearing clothes that someone else has chosen for you; it's another thing altogether to stand next to the model-like figure of Saffron while you're doing it. She made it all seem so easy. I was mortified, and it showed. The pictures came back and Saffron naturally looks like a goddess. I, on the other hand, look like the poor unfortunate who's missed the last bus home.'

While this was told as another self-deprecating joke, there are, of course, elements of truth in it. Her self-image is far from positive and no amount of fame or flattery seems to boost her self-esteem – or at least she will never admit to it publicly. But she has been lauded from the rooftops by her contemporaries, fellow comics and major international stars, which surely must allow her to feel some sort of warm glow.

*

It was Dawn French who first started the ball rolling after they starred together in BBC1 sitcom *Wild West*. Her paraphrased quote, which has been used extensively, was: 'Catherine Tate is very, very funny and may have to be destroyed.' After this, it seemed to be open season on telling Tate just how great she was. Richard Curtis, the man behind *Blackadder*, *Notting Hill* and *Love Actually*, came up to her after the BAFTAs and told her she was the cleverest comedienne working today. The founder of the fund-raising *Comic Relief* which Tate was to become so heavily involved with later, Curtis' opinion was certainly to be taken seriously.

Much-respected writer and comic actor Simon Pegg, he of cult sitcom *Spaced* and hit movies *Shaun Of The Dead* and *Hot Fuzz*, waded in with: 'Catherine is perhaps the most gifted character actress of her generation – intuitive, versatile and hilarious.'

Northern comic God Peter Kay, whose *Phoenix Nights* series, set in a working men's club, will remain forever a classic, is equally flattering. Having worked with her early in both their careers in *That Peter Kay Thing* in 1999 he said: 'I knew straight away she was a remarkable talent. I always think it's like a spark that comedians see in each other, and for me Catherine has the talent that I've only ever seen before in Julie Walters in that her character portrayals are so believable and funny.' A decidedly down-to-earth and unstarry man himself, he also says that Tate is one of the few true friends he has made in the 'celebrity' world, and the two of them get together whenever she's in Manchester.

In the realms of megastar fans, there are two from the world of music who stand out. One is George Michael, who famously joined her for her last Christmas special, abandoning all his dignity to play a hospital patient who ends up being snogged by sex-mad Bernie. He had already asked her to compere a benefit gig for NHS nurses which he had organized, and had admitted to the press that he played DVDs of *The Catherine Tate Show* before his live performances to psyche himself up. 'I watch her show to warm me up. I love it,' he said. She received the ultimate high-profile pat on the back when he interrupted one of his sell-out Earls Court gigs to shine a spotlight on her in the audience. Informing his fans that she was 'the soundtrack of my tour' caused some 30,000 people to cheer.

The other pop legend to gain succour from Tate's comedy creations is none other than gay icon herself, Kylie Minogue. Australian born Minogue, former star of Aussie soap *Neighbours,* had become an international star as a pop singer with a huge run of hits. Held in high public esteem, the general public seemed devastated when it was announced that she was suffering from breast cancer. Sister Dannii Minogue revealed that, while Kylie was undergoing treatment for breast cancer, it was *The Catherine Tate Show* that kept her going. 'We've been loving Catherine Tate for a while now and we can both do brilliant impressions of Lauren the schoolgirl. It's really keeping Kylie going right now.' All those old adages about laughter being the best medicine clearly hold true.

GMTV presenter Fiona Phillips also paid Tate and Lauren the ultimate compliment by getting done up as the latter for a magazine photo-shoot. As a fan of the show, she said that she really identified with the rebellious big-mouth. 'Dressing up as Lauren took me back to my own childhood. I went to quite a rough school and I confess I was a lot like her as a schoolgirl. I thought it was great that Catherine stayed in character to talk to the Queen and Prince Philip when she met them recently. She's only acting and the Royal Family shouldn't be treated any differently. I'm sure they have a sense of humour don't they?'

Whether they did or not was tested by Catherine's appearance as Lauren at the Royal Variety Performance, which is discussed elsewhere. But to know that the Royal Family are aware of your existence, and are familiar with your work, must be quite a buzz. As must going to Number Ten Downing Street and performing a sketch with the prime minister. And, given Tate's *Friends* obsession, having Jennifer Aniston pop backstage when she performed in *The 24 Hour Plays* on Broadway in New York probably sent her into paroxysms of self-conscious glee. This production had started at the Old Vic in London and been transferred to America's most revered theatrical street.

In terms of career though, it is the opinions of those with whom you work most closely that really count. Geoffrey Perkins, the man she collaborated with on all three sketch shows, and formerly Head of Comedy for the BBC, has nothing but praise for his star. Having worked with her to develop her stand-up characters into fully-rounded television creations, he was excited, despite her lack of profile.

'Nobody knew who Catherine was at first so it was a hard show to publicize. Success was certainly not guaranteed. But people love it because it's so well observed. She has a very good ear for real dialogue and captures the minute details of characters, and that's what makes them so recognizable and believable. Catherine is a brilliant actress, too – she makes becoming all those people look easy. When she's performing she's very sharp and focused. She knows what it means to have her own show; to be the one in charge – it's a big deal and she always wants it to be perfect.'

He also warns those who may be foolish enough to underestimate the quiet star: 'She can appear quiet but you mustn't underestimate her. When she's focused on something, she's a *tour de force*. She describes herself as a lazy control freak. But when the time comes to do it, she changes. Her brain moves incredibly fast when she's performing.'

Could anyone want a better reference from a boss? With these kinds of glowing recommendations, it's unsurprising that Tate is fielding tempting offers from the worlds of television, film and theatre. Feted by many, and courted by more, she is still rightly cautious of the torrent of good fortune that seems to have descended on her head.

Interviewing her for the *Radio Times*, fellow comedian Alexei Sayle professed himself worried that the softly spoken woman he met wouldn't be able to cope with such attention and wealth she was now receiving. 'Feeling the vibe of excitement and the smell of money that surrounds her,' he wrote, 'it occurs to me that, finally, comedians may have achieved the status of rock stars. In fact, better than rock stars, because rock stars are mostly young, vain idiots and Catherine Tate seems like a nice, normal woman, admittedly one who's tremendously entertaining, both in person and on TV.'

This kind man, who had tasted his own share of fame and fortune in the 1980s, felt he wanted to look after her. Given her natural caution, strong family ties and sensible attitude to all things celebrity, it's pretty likely that Catherine Tate can probably take care of herself.

CHAPTER FIFTEEN

Awards

While Catherine Tate has won a smattering of awards throughout her television comedy career, it's fair to say that her shelves aren't as full as they might have been. Nominated for no less than five British Academy of Film and Television Awards (BAFTAs), she has lost out each time, and in 2007 failed to hide her disgust at missing out to *That Mitchell And Webb Look* in the category of Best Comedy Programme or Series.

A sketch show very similar in format to *The Catherine Tate Show*, it mostly parodied television genres. Sketches included 'Numberwang' which portrayed a ridiculous gameshow and bore a passing resemblance to *Countdown* albeit if the contestants had taken sedatives before agreeing to take part, a pair of ageing and useless snooker commentators called Ted and Peter, and 'Big Talk', which featured a panel of boffins trying to solve the problems of the day. Given the popularity of her three series, and the fact that this was the third time she'd got dolled up to attend this rather glitzy ceremony only to come home empty-handed, it's hard not to sympathize with her.

She had fared slightly better at the British Comedy Awards, the annual booze-up for the great and good in the comedy world, which usually happens in December and is hosted by Jonathan Ross and televized on ITV1. Here she won an award for Best Comedy Newcomer in 2004 and Best TV Comedy Actress in 2006 and was rubbing shoulders with the cream of Britain's comedy talent from Lucas and Walliams to Harry Hill, Ricky Gervais, Stephen Merchant, French and Saunders and Sacha Baron Cohen.

However, in 2005 she had come home empty-handed, failing to pick up both the Best Comedy Actress Award and the People's Choice Award, as voted for by the viewing public. That can't have been a very cheery evening for her, and she would have to wait nearly two and a half years to discover that the People's Choice Award should have been in the back of her cab that night, rather than in the clutches of Geordie entertainment duo, Ant and Dec. From acting in children's drama *Byker Grove* through to presenting some of ITV's most watched and talked about shows such as *I'm A Celebrity, Get Me Out Of Here*, Ant McPartlin and Declan Donnelly were, and still are, Britain's most popular television faces.

This was sensationally revealed in April 2008, when an investigation by legal firm Olswang concluded that Tate, rather than Ant and Dec, should have gone home with the award, as she received more telephone votes than Ant and Dec's show *Saturday Night Takeaway*. The People's Choice Award is the only British Comedy Award that is not decided on by a panel, and is supposedly given to the person who receives the most phone and text votes from the British public. Previous winners have included sitcom *One Foot In The Grave*, comedy drama *Cold Feet*, *Peter Kay's Phoenix Nights* and *Little Britain*.

The tale that emerged was labyrinthine and firmly in the category of 'you couldn't make it up'. It seemed the pop superstar Robbie Williams had agreed to present an award at the ceremony, but only if it could be guaranteed that it would be to his old friends, Ant McPartlin and Declan Donnelly. The three of them reportedly play football together whenever they're all in Los Angeles. So far, so showbiz cosy. The problem seemed to be that Ant and Dec hadn't won any of the awards already decided on by the panel of judges, and the only award left was The People's Choice Award. But it seemed that the people weren't going to be able to choose.

During the first part of the ceremony, broadcast before the *ITV News*, *The Catherine Tate Show* had garnered more votes that *Saturday Night Takeaway*, but, while the show was off-air, Ant and Dec were announced to be the winners to the live audience. To add insult to injury, viewers who continued to watch the Awards after the *News* were persuaded that the show was 'as live', and were encouraged to continue voting, even though the award had already been handed over. They were thus handing over hard-earned money, via expensive phone lines, to participate in a vote they had no possible hope of influencing.

This fiasco was announced on the same day in April 2008 that broadcasting regulator OFCOM fined ITV £5.7 million for repeatedly misleading viewers over the conduct of phone-ins on *Ant And Dec's Saturday Night Takeaway*, *Ant And Dec's Gameshow Marathon* and *Soapstar Superstar*. The latter show saw cast members of various soap operas trying to persuade judges and viewers of their singing talents. Viewers had spent £7.8 million making phone calls to the three shows at up to £1 a time, entering competitions that were rigged. Contestants on *Ant and Dec's Saturday Night Takeaway* had been chosen on the basis of where they lived and, in the case of *Ant And Dec's Gameshow Marathon,* on how 'lively' they sounded, while *Soapstar Superstar* repeatedly overrode the choice of songs voted for by viewers in January 2007. The sanction was the largest OFCOM had ever imposed on a broadcaster and 'reflects not only the seriousness of ITV's failures but also their repeated nature.'

So it was severe egg-on-face time not only for ITV but for the hugely popular presenting duo who, up until these revelations, had seemed unable to do any wrong. ITV's most bankable stars, Ant and Dec, had been ratings winners for the network at a time when it had been struggling to maintain its place in a multi-channel world. The Olswang investigation found no evidence that the presenters or their mate, Robbie Williams, were aware of what had happened. Ant and Dec professed themselves 'completely shocked' when the news came out and promised to return their award. Everything was not clear cut though, as the report said: 'While it can be concluded that the assurance was given to ensure Robbie Williams' attendance to present an award, it cannot be concluded that this was the reason why the wrong winner of the People's Choice Award was announced.'

The row continued to rumble on, as later newspaper reports said that it wasn't definite that Catherine Tate should have won the award rather than Ant and Dec. Claiming that the Olswang report was inconclusive, Paul Pascoe, director of Michael Hurll Television, the company that had produced the British Comedy Awards since their inception, said: 'We are still trying to find out if they won the award because it's not certain Catherine Tate should have won it. We discovered last July a question mark as to whether they should have won and brought it to ITV's attention. As far as everyone is concerned Catherine Tate should have won, and Ant and Dec are probably taking that to be the gospel truth too. At the moment, we have seen two results one saying Ant and Dec won, and the other saying Catherine Tate won.'

A separate OFCOM investigation was launched to put the matter to rest. As Pascoe said: 'What we would like to see is the raw data from the phone company, which will include the data from the text vote, online vote and phone vote, and that's down to OFCOM to track down. We are hugely embarrassed and confused by all of this.'

While the OFCOM investigation was still ongoing, an ITV spokesman did say: 'Catherine Tate was the clear winner of the People's Choice British Comedy Award in 2005.' Ant and Dec, however, had still not handed over the award, and their spokesman explained: 'The boys would never want to receive an award under the circumstances that arose in the ITV report and they are waiting to see the result of OFCOM's report.'

Whichever way you look at it, this was an unholy mess. Tate must surely have permitted herself a private laugh at this cock-up of epic proportions but she very wisely declined to comment on any of the stories at the time. Sometimes a dignified silence is the only way to go.

Tate may have been robbed at the British Comedy Awards and serially snubbed at the posher BAFTAs, but there were other bodies that saw fit to reward her talents. She swept the board at the Royal Television Society Awards in 2006, winning Best Network Newcomer, Best Comedy Performance and Best Entertainment Programme. And, in the National Television Awards of 2007, all voted for by the public rather than a panel of 'experts', she took the gong for Most Popular Comedy Programme.

Tate didn't turn up at the ceremony herself, instead choosing to nominate her friend Philip Glenister to collect it for her. The star of *Life On Mars* had just filmed his part in her Christmas Special of 2007. He sent Catherine's thanks and apologies for not attending as she was 'babysitting Trevor McDonald's children'. The newscaster and documentary maker was hosting the show. Given her hatred of awards ceremonies and red carpets, and her visible disappointment at other events, she probably decided it was best not to risk showing her face. It was ironic that the award was presented by Matt Lucas and David Walliams, done up as their *Little Britain* characters Lou and Andy, as she had lost out to that show so many times before. It could have been quite a sweet moment, face to face. Had she slipped into Nan on stage, that old harridan would surely have dispatched this hapless pair with their tails between their legs.

There were happier moments, such as in 2004, when she picked up the Best Newcomer Award at the British Comedy Awards beating off James McAvoy from *Shameless* and Noel Fielding and Julian Barratt from *The Mighty Boosh*. Her first major award, she hadn't been prepared to take to the stage as the winner. As she later explained: 'I couldn't believe it. I'd booked a cab for about one minute after the ceremony so I couldn't do any standing around doing any "My God, I've won!" stuff. Though I did have some Kettle Chips.'

It's probably just as well, as the British Comedy Awards after-show party is notorious for its hardcore boozing. Having spent all evening in a hot television studio guzzling wine, the cooped-up comedy stars then hit the disco at an upstairs room in London Television Centre on the South Bank of the Thames. The scenes that follow aren't usually pretty and, given Tate's complete abstinence from alcohol, she might have found them hard to deal with. Although, come to think of it, they could have provided her with a wealth of new comedy material.

She might have had a moment of sober reflection on the Newcomer Award too, if she had caught Johnny Vegas's hilarious presentation speech a couple of years earlier. The northern comedian, who now appears in the PG Tips ads with the famous monkey was himself the recipient the year before of the Best Newcomer Award. He came on to present an award and, in a drunken and hilarious speech, said that it only took twelve months to go from Best Newcomer to embittered has-been, adding that, 'It's only a slightly slower demise than *Popstars*.' He was referring to yet another ITV talent show that attempted to manufacture girl and boy bands. While Girls Aloud did rather well out of this, its other alumni such as Hear'Say, One True Voice and Phixx fared less well.

Tate's lack of BAFTA success after five nominations is clearly a sore point for the actress and comedian. Nominated for Best

New Writer and Best Comedy Programme in 2005, Best Comedy Performance and Best Comedy Programme in 2006, and then Best Comedy Programme in 2007, she came away from every ceremony empty-handed.

On her way into the BAFTAs in 2007 she walked the red carpet and engaged in a number of interviews with TV reporters. When asked if she practised her faces for winning and losing, she quipped: 'I haven't got a happy face'. She wasn't lying, as will be explained later. She went on to tell the reporter, in a burst of absolute honesty: 'I've just lost too many times. I'll be livid if I lose, don't get me wrong. It won't be directed at the people who have won. I will be really disappointed if I haven't won *again*, believe me.'

And so it came to pass that David Mitchell and Robert Webb were announced the winners for *That Mitchell And Webb Look*. Tate was as livid as she'd promised she'd be and her expression of disgust was caught on camera for the whole world to see. You can even relive the moment on YouTube if you missed out the first time.

Commentators were gleeful to catch such an honest reaction as most losers have spent hours practising their happy reactions, and put on a brave face no matter how much they may be seething internally with rage at the injustice of it all. Clare Margetson, the Arts Editor of the *Guardian,* writing in her blog the next day, commented on how any acting training had gone out of the window not only for Tate but for actor John Simm too who co-starred with Philip Glenister in *Life On Mars*: 'John Simm looked more and more glum as *Life On Mars* lost out on Best Drama Series and Best Actor (though thankfully it did eventually win the Audience Award). But did you see the look on Catherine Tate's face – her mouth plunging to her chest – when Mitchell and Webb took Best Comedy Award? Was she bovvered? You betcha.'

Tate even felt moved to complain afterwards, telling a *Mirror* reporter when she was a guest at the Ivor Novello Awards for songwriting: 'I don't like to use the word fixed but it should be fair. Only ten people vote but have they asked the nation? I've lost three times.' Maybe it was being at another awards ceremony, albeit one in which she had no hope of nomination or triumph, that set her off.

When asked in a questionnaire what her most unappealing habit was, her answer was: 'Pouting. I don't realize I'm doing it.' Perhaps this is what happened at the BAFTAs. It might have looked like sour grapes and done her reputation little good, but at least it demonstrates her honesty in the face of adversity.

She'd reportedly been almost as fed up at the previous year's BAFTAs when she lost out to BBC2 sitcom *Help* in Best Comedy Programme, and to Chris Langham in *The Thick Of It* for Best Comedy Performance. *Little Britain* was also nominated in the Best Comedy Programme and Matt Lucas said this at the time, as reported in Boyd Hilton's book, *Inside Little Britain*: 'We can't possibly win. It would be incredible. I think Catherine Tate will win. She deserves it. She keeps missing out and it's outrageous really.'

When Tate failed to win either award she was up for, Lucas and partner Walliams went to commiserate and she didn't hide her disillusionment. Lucas, a former colleague on the stand-up circuit, said he was angry on her behalf.

While the BAFTA panel is, of course, entitled to its opinions, it was beginning to look like a deliberate snub after five nominations, and Tate's frustration was understandable. *Father Ted* creator Arthur Mathews doesn't think you can put it down to snobbery though: 'She's picked up a lot of other awards, I know. To be honest, I think that it's just a knife edge decision. There'd be no reason for people to give an award to *Little Britain* as opposed to Catherine Tate. They're both very mainstream shows and you couldn't say it was a snobbish decision. Mitchell and Webb are fantastic and I think they were due a lot of awards. You might find that Catherine starts winning a lot of things now. She could probably start picking up stuff for *Doctor Who*. She's terrific in that as well and looks perfectly at home in it.'

When asked about her surprising lack of awards success by *Heat* magazine in December 2006, she had managed to put a far braver face on it: 'To be honest, it's always very sweet that people say that. I mean, Paul O'Grady [Liverpudlian comedian and television presenter who now hosts his own teatime show on Channel 4] rants on about it and I think it's so sweet that people notice. But genuinely, I ain't bovvered! You know, I think I'm the most popular loser! It's fantastic because I get the biggest cheers when I lose. What I care about is that people like the show and that the show's been well received.' She may well have meant this when she said it, but a few months later the mask of happy and gracious loser had well and truly slipped.

Still, there were other accolades to be had away from the BAFTAs. In November 2005, she was named number three in the prestigious *Broadcast* magazine's Top 100 of the UK's top television talent. The only people to beat her were David Tennant who had recently taken over as the Doctor in *Doctor Who* and campaigning cheeky-chap chef, Jamie Oliver. Coming in below her in descending order were Bill Oddie, Ant and Dec, Paul O'Grady, Julia Davis of *Nighty Night* fame, *Top Gear*'s Richard Hammond, Mitchell and Webb, and comedian Hardeep Singh Kohli. The list was announced shortly after her show-stealing sketch at the Royal Variety Performance in which she asked the Queen, 'Is one bovvered?'

The following year saw her in the line-up of a poll commissioned by the *Radio Times* to find the top ten funny women of all time. Veteran comedian and actress Victoria Wood took the top spot with Tate's co-star from *Wild West*, Dawn French, coming in at number two. French was described in the *Radio Times* as a 'great big playful pixie with a God-given gift for clowning'. Kathy Burke, whom Tate pressed into service as Nan's daughter, Diane, was at number three and was described as being able to make the grotesque oddly appealing. The rest of the top ten was made up of Julie Walters, Jennifer Saunders, Jo Brand, Joyce Grenfell, Joan Rivers, Lucille Ball, and Tate herself. She came in at number nine, ahead of Lucille Ball. To join such august company must have been a delight for Tate. She had already described French, Saunders, Wood and Walters as 'idols'. And once, when asked which living person she most admired, she said: 'Anyone who stands up for themselves and others – as long as they're not annoying about it. And Joan Rivers.' With this endorsement, she had truly joined the comedy cognoscenti.

Let us not forget that 'bovvered' was pronounced Word Of

The Year in 2006 by the people behind the Oxford English Dictionary, and she also received a Canadian Rockie (given out at the annual Banff World Television Awards) for Best Comedy in 2004, as well as an international Emmy nomination for Best Performance By An Actress in 2005.

There may still be gaps on her mantelpiece, but, given the seriousness with which she is taking her future career, they may not be empty for too much longer.

CHAPTER SIXTEEN

No Compromise

As a child, Catherine Tate used to sit with a weighted riding hat on her head, attempting to straighten her naturally curly red hair. Now, with some of the world's leading make-up and hair experts on hand, she can have her red locks straightened and blow dried to perfection whenever she wants. It may be a hoary old cliché but the girl from the inner London council estate has come an awful long way. Geographically, she may have only moved a few miles from Bloomsbury to Mortlake in south-west London, but even her most fantastical girlish dreaming can't have imagined the level of fame and success she would go on to achieve.

Her accomplishments must be all the more satisfying for having taken a lot of time and hard work to achieve. Not blessed with the sculpted good looks of a natural leading lady, Tate didn't fall out of drama school straight into the lead ingénue role in the West End. Nor was she courted for high-profile television roles that required gamine teens. But she persevered through thankless years of bit parts in long-running TV dramas, played countless spear carriers and whores at the National Theatre and the RSC, and somehow found the strength to keep going until she found her true talents. Her move from straight acting to stand-up comedy was an inspired one, allowing her both to develop her natural flair for comedy and get seen by some of the most important people in the industry. Whatever she might say about her lack of ambition, there has to be some iron in the soul if you're to put yourself through these terror-inducing trials.

While her talent was eventually spotted at the Edinburgh Festival and capitalized on quite quickly, she was no overnight success. Given her ambivalence towards fame, it's just as well that it came at the relatively late stage of her mid-thirties: any sooner and the effects could have been catastrophic. Given that her very first television sketch show had her name all over it, it was obvious that the limelight was inevitable. She apparently fought this decision at the time though: 'Right at the beginning I said I wasn't mad about calling it *The Catherine Tate Show*, from the coward's point of view, because if people don't like it they're just going to look at the title and go, "That show's shit and so is she." But you can't have something without my name on it and then me get all the best parts, so we had to use it. Obviously, when people like the show, the spotlight does go disproportionately on me, but that's the chance you take.'

It was a chance that paid off handsomely as her blend of character comedy, sharp writing and memorable performances made an instant impact on the public. The catchphrases, whether she wrote them knowingly or not, also helped enormously. As everyone from your local landlord to old ladies at bus stops started asking, 'Am I bovvered though?' or exclaiming, 'How very dare you!', it quickly felt like Tate had been part of the comedy scene forever. As the producer of *The Catherine Tate Show*, Geoffrey Perkins, observed: 'Catherine is quite difficult to pigeon hole. It's what she does. She arrived looking like she'd been around for years and years.'

While this self-assurance might have come across on screen in broad, confident characterization, behind the scenes it was, of course, a very different story. It's astonishing to watch the first two series of *The Catherine Tate Show* now and realize that she was suffering from severe postnatal depression during both the writing and recording of them. How can you possibly be this funny when you're experiencing depression?

What might have helped her pull off this remarkable feat is the fact that the shows were such a natural extension of the characters and comedy she'd been developing on the stand-up circuit. As Bruce Dessau, comedy critic of the *Evening Standard* and former Perrier Award judge, observes: 'When Catherine Tate did her first solo show at the Edinburgh Festival it was like a low-budget, prosthetic-free dry fun for her BBC series. It was the first time I'd seen her and it was clear she was going to make it. All the building blocks were in place for a successful character comedy as she switched personae at the drop of a shoestring prop. One moment she was a raunchy nurse, the next a sozzled bride insulting the assembled wedding guests. It was clear that this was a performer with wide appeal and huge prospects. While some Edinburgh acts would be destined for cult status, Tate had mainstream stardom running through her like words through a stick of rock.'

Not having to compromize her original ideas in order to make it big in television must have helped. Impostor syndrome, so called because of a person's belief that they're about to be tapped on the shoulder and told to go back to their old life because they're a fraud, is very common in successful people. The fact that Tate was developing her natural talents rather than being shoe-horned into some television producer's vision of mainstream comedy should have minimized this. Her discomfort for the celebrity lifestyle was obvious from the beginning, and it was clear that she hadn't really thought through the impact on her life of having a successful BBC series with her name on it. Celebrity was something that she gazed at rather than dreamed of joining, as this answer to what her guilty pleasure was, before the launch of her first series, shows: 'Celebrity magazines. I feel a bit sick with myself for buying so many. I'm obsessed with celebrity in an unclean way. I feel disdain for celebrities and I'm quite snobbish about what they get up to. But I can't wait to rush out and read all about them. I love looking at the unflattering photos.'

Having been such an avid consumer of the products she was now forced to feature in, she understood their ghastly appeal. No wonder it made her feel slightly sick that she herself was now fair game for the 'Circle of Shame'. Having felt disdain for celebrities, did she now feel disdain for herself at joining their ranks?

Her well-documented struggle with the limelight would seem to confirm this, although she did scrub up beautifully for the 2007 BAFTAs in a plunging black frock and gamely braved the red carpet. The honesty of her remarks as she did so told us that she was never going to be entirely comfortable playing the fame game.

*

Having turned forty in May 2008, Tate may well have used this traditional milestone to reflect on her life. Let's hope that she allowed herself some congratulations for what she has achieved and didn't entirely indulge her 'glass-half-empty' personality. In a stable relationship for the last eight years with partner Twig Clark, the mother of a healthy five-year-old daughter and adored by her mother and other close family, she has the solid foundations for happiness, even putting aside her career. Having toured the universe with the lovely *Doctor Who* on BBC1 every Saturday night, she is now starring in yet another highbrow West End play, and writing a drama for a prestigious BBC project, and it seems certain that she will never allow herself to rest on her laurels.

The BBC project is called *Decades*, thirty one-hour dramas written by thirty different writers focusing on the last thirty-five years. Eager to accept a new challenge, she was nonetheless worried about delivering such an ambitious idea: 'It's one of those things that I really hope I see through. All I am really interested in is character and dialogue. It's plot that I fear I may fall down on.'

The play was David Eldridge's love story *Under The Blue Sky* at the Duke Of York's Theatre in the West End where she joined Francesca Annis and Chris O'Dowd to put herself through another work-out on stage, and subjected herself to more criticism, this time of the theatrical variety. But after *Doctor Who*, it was a natural progression to return to what first drove her career. As she told the *Radio Times* in 2006: 'I'd love to do more theatre. That's probably my first love, and I'd love to do more drama, but comedy is what I feel in my bones. I don't feel I will stay away from comedy for very long hopefully.'

Whether it's more of *The Catherine Tate Show* or something entirely different, Tate will hopefully be making us laugh again before too long. Her desperation not to get pigeon holed and her low threshold for boredom may stop her from returning to her well-loved characters, but she hasn't entirely ruled it out.

'There is a tendency to bracket people. I mix things up and do different stuff or I get bored. But I love doing my show. I loved doing it when I was playing to sixty people in Edinburgh, so doing it on this scale is incredible. But what I have to realize is that, if I'm not careful, that'll be the only thing people want to see me do, and I'd be reluctant fifteen years down the line to still be trotting it out. Listen, I'll be lucky if in fifteen years people remember it at all. Don't get me wrong, but I'm just aware there are hopefully lots of other things to do, and I don't want it to outstay its welcome. And I don't want to run out of ideas.'

Having made her mark as Donna Noble in *Doctor Who*, and trodden the boards of the West End, she may well feel safe enough to return to Nan et al before long. She seemed to confirm this, at least tentatively, in May 2008 when a BBC interviewer asked her if she would continue with the show: 'If I have more ideas I will… we need to have some new ideas, then hopefully yes.'

With her talents encompassing straight acting, brilliant comic timing and both the writing and performance of highly memorable characters, Tate has a lot to draw on for her future career. With her penchant for picking out very different projects – she took a meeting to consider writing *Baywatch: The Musical* – we may well be in for some big surprises.

Whatever happens next, she has created a lasting legacy with her pantheon of comic characters. However much she might protest that people may not even remember who she is ten years down the line, Lauren, Nan and Derek, at least, will stay in the national psyche for some considerable time to come. They may well be haunting our nightmares as well as making us laugh via our DVD players, but they are nothing if not unforgettable.

As for Catherine Tate, when asked how she'd like to be remembered, she said: 'As an old woman who died peacefully in her sleep at 106.' That gives her another sixty-six years of creative life to play with. Let's hope she continues to play for as long as she possibly can.

Acknowledgements

Articles from the following periodicals, wire services and websites assisted the researching of this book: *The Independent*, *The Guardian*, *Daily Mirror*, *The Times*, *The Sunday Times*, *The Daily Telegraph*, *Radio Times*, *Heat*, *Closer*, *Daily Mail*, *The Works*, *The Sun*, *TV Quick*, *The Daily Star*, *TV Times*, *Daily Express*, *News Of The World*, *Elle*, *Sunday Mirror*, *Woman*, *The Sunday Sun*, WENN, *Evening Standard*, *The Irish News*, *Broadcast*, *The Observer*, *Coventry Evening Telegraph*, *The Mail On Sunday*, *Sunday Express*, *Daily Record*, bumpnotfrump.com, *South Wales Echo*, *The Spectator*, *Time Out*, *Staff Brand Republic*, *The Sunday Telegraph*, *The Western Mail*, *The People*, *New Statesman*, *The Edinburgh Evening News*, bbc.co.uk, *Inside Little Britain*, imdb.com.

Index

Note: the page numbers in **bold** are major references